Hear Us, Good Lord

Lenten Meditations from
Washington National Cathedral

D1165957

FORWARD MOVEMENT
Cincinnati, Ohio

Introduction

The Great Litany is one of the richest liturgical offerings of the church. At Washington National Cathedral, this intercessory prayer is chanted in procession throughout the nave, side aisles, and transepts of our sacred space during Lent each year. To hear these ancient prayer petitions chanted by a solo voice followed by the sung responses of all gathered in that vast space is quite poignant and impactful.

The Great Litany was first used as early as the fifth century in Rome, later modified by Archbishop Thomas Cranmer, and first published in English in 1544. Although the litany's use and language have evolved over the centuries, our need for repentance, forgiveness, and amendment of life remain unchanged.

This book is a collection of meditations written by cathedral staff, lay and clergy, and friends of the cathedral. The authors are a diverse group, as you will see from the short biographies at the end of the book. We hope you will find that our diversity brings new perspectives and epiphanies to you in your own spiritual journey. This book also marks our second book collaboration with our friends at Forward Movement. We were delighted to partner with them for Lent 2022 with *The Pilgrim Way of Lent: Reflections from Washington National Cathedral.* Forward Movement has spiritually nurtured generations of Christians since 1935, and we are once again honored to partner with them in this spiritual offering.

As you read and reflect upon each petition, meditation, and prayer in this book, we hope your spiritual journey will be deepened and enriched. These ancient petitions have accompanied Christians on their pilgrimage of faith for more than 500 years. We join a great cloud of witnesses as we too walk the way of Jesus.

May God bless and keep you.

THE VERY REV. RANDOLPH MARSHALL HOLLERITH
DEAN OF WASHINGTON NATIONAL CATHEDRAL

Ash Wednesday

Ash Wednesday

O God the Father, Creator of heaven and earth,

Have mercy upon us.

The story of creation in the book of Genesis does not contain many facts, but it is full of truth. The world was not created in seven days and the cosmology of our ancestors, who wrote the creation story, is far from what we know now about our world and the nature of the universe. Yet, the story of creation is a sacred story, full of poetry, that tells us some very important truths about the world and our place in it. The first and most important truth is that our God, who created the heavens and the earth, made everything good. Repeatedly throughout the seven days of creation—whether God was separating the dry land from the sea, creating the sun and the moon, or bringing forth plants, animals, and human beings—Genesis tells us that everything God made was good. In this sense, a great truth of our faith is that you and I and everything on this planet and in our universe was created to be good. We were made in love by the God of love and that can only be good.

At the same time, Genesis tells us a second truth, that sin is a fundamental reality of our world. Something happened, and we turned away from God's goodness. Adam and Eve, the snake, and the apple are not historical facts, but the story of the fall is deeply true. We live in a world that is awash in sin, and sin is separation. We are separated from God. We are separated from creation. We are separated from one another; we are separated from our best selves. Sin is that which breaks apart all these relationships, and while it is sin that separates, it is love that reconciles and reunites.

Ash Wednesday is when we own up to the reality of sin in our world and in our selves. We acknowledge that we do not live as God our creator intended. We repent of our broken relationships with God, the world, each other, and ourselves. And we are reminded of our complete dependence on the God who created us from the dust of the earth. As we begin the Lenten journey, let us consciously turn away from the sin that drives us apart and commit ourselves to the love of God that, as Saint Paul reminds us in his letter to the Ephesians, seeks to gather together in one all things in Christ, both in heaven and on earth.

—Randolph Marshall Hollerith

Almighty and everlasting God, you hate nothing you have made and forgive the sins of all who are penitent: Create and make in us new and contrite hearts, that we, worthily lamenting our sins and acknowledging our wretchedness, may obtain of you, the God of all mercy, perfect remission and forgiveness; through Jesus Christ our Lord, who lives and reigns with you and the Holy Spirit, one God, for ever and ever. Amen.

—The Book of Common Prayer, p.264

Thursday after Ash Wednesday ___

O, God the Son, Redeemer of the world,

Have mercy upon us.

I wonder how to pray the Great Litany as a daily spiritual practice during Lent. The whole litany is long and wordy, written as a call-and-response prayer. But a short rubric at the beginning of the liturgical text offers the perfect advice about how to engage with this profound prayer: "to be said or sung, kneeling, standing, or in procession" (The Book of Common Prayer, p. 148).

I wonder how transformative it would be to pray this litany in daily procession, while walking to work or school or during a hiking session or a family walk around the neighborhood. I wonder what new understanding of the world around us would come as a result of walking while praying: "O, God the Son, Redeemer of the world, have mercy upon us." How would it be to engage with the world in that way while intentionally seeing and walking around?

The idea would be to walk while "reading" our reality in need of God the Son's redemption. Our neighbors' lives, institutions, and local businesses, creation, visitors, and strangers wandering outdoors, our whole small world...all brought up in our prayer, being seen mercifully by Christ, our Redeemer. Such a daily pilgrimage using the Great Litany could be a perfect spiritual exercise during this Lent.

Maybe this could be an opportunity to notice in new ways how God the Son reveals God's self in the brokenness and intricacies of our own small world in which we live. Everything needs Christ's redemptive love experienced in full at the cross. From there, the world is more than sin, deception, and chaos. From the redemptive experience of the cross, Christ transforms what is broken into wholeness, bringing all what we are and all our realities to God. Redemption is liberation, salvation, and communion—all made possible by Christ, our Lord. Which areas of your life are in need of redemption? Which areas of your world are screaming for Christ's redemption right now? Name them while wandering, using the words of this litany and your own words.

I can imagine this type of prayer could transform not only our world but also ourselves, opening our eyes, awakening our bodies, and connecting our souls with the divine.

I wonder while wandering.

—Yoimel González Hernández

You have given all to me.
To you, Lord, I return it.
Everything is yours; do with it what you will.
Give me only your love and your grace,
that is enough for me. Amen.

—Saint Ignatius of Loyola

Friday after Ash Wednesday_____

O God the Holy Ghost, Sanctifier of the faithful,

Have mercy upon us.

"I still have many things to say to you, but you cannot bear them now. When the Spirit of truth comes, he will guide you into all the truth."

—John 16:12-13a (English Standard Version)

Many Christians are nervous when talking about the Holy Spirit. Most anyone can take a stab at describing God the Father (think Creator) and God the Son (Jesus), but God the Holy Spirit is elusive and vague—like wind, a breath, a flame, a descending dove.

If the Trinity is the church's shorthand for the myriad ways we can and do experience God, then God the Father is that collection of attributes and actions that reveal God's almost-parental love for and plan for all of creation. God the Son is what happened when God chose to reveal God's self dramatically in the life of one finite human being, when God gave up all the prerogatives of being God to experience what it's like to be one of us.

What then are we to make of the Holy Spirit? It's hard to define the Holy Spirit, and that is as it should be, because the Holy Spirit is the part of God that won't be tied down, confined to anyone's definition, or neatly tied up in a package. The Holy Spirit is the "wild side" of God—the often-surprising actions taken by the Living God to be in relationship with us.

At the Last Supper, Jesus spends part of his last precious bit of time with the disciples to tell them to expect the Holy Spirit. He admits to them that his work isn't finished with them. And why? They are simply unable to bear all that he wants to teach and impart to them. God's solution to that incompleteness is the Holy Spirit, which will, over time (lots of time), teach us everything God wants us to know. The Holy Spirit will lead us into all the truth, sanctifying us, making us more like God, day by day.

If they could have borne it, wouldn't the disciples have learned from Jesus that enslaving another human being is always wrong? If the culture could have even imagined such a thing, wouldn't Jesus have told them about respecting the dignity of every human being, starting with the valuing of women? If the disciples could have grasped the complexity of human sexuality, wouldn't Jesus have taught them about LGBT, gender-nonconforming, and queer people, and God's love for them? But since they could not bear it, that sanctification would become the future work of the Holy Spirit.

What truth is the Holy Spirit wanting to teach you this Lent? Buckle up! It might be a wild ride!

GENE ROBINSON

O Holy Spirit God, blow into my life like a fresh wind, stay as close as my breath, set my heart afire with your love for others, and give me the peace of a descending dove. Open me up to whatever truth you want to lead me into today. Give me the courage to embrace your wild Spirit in my life, to your honor and glory. Amen.

Saturday after Ash Wednesday ___

O holy, blessed, and glorious Trinity, one God,

Have mercy upon us.

"How do I love thee? Let me count the ways." These much-quoted opening words from Sonnet 43, written by Elizabeth Barrett Browning to her husband Robert Browning, are the words that come to my mind when I think of the Trinity. Just as they signal a love poem in which Elizabeth expresses the breadth and depth of her love for her husband, they suggest for us a love dance in which God reveals the fullness and steadfastness of God's love for us. To speak of God as Trinity is to express the ways in which our one God loves us. How does God love us? Let me count the ways.

God loves us as a creator—breathing us into life as God's very children. God loves us as a Savior—freeing us from the sins that betray and alienate us from the sacredness of our very creation. God loves us as an advocate—forever guiding us in the way of truth and peace that is God's promise to us all. Hence, we have traditionally proclaimed our one God as Father, Son and Holy Spirit. Essentially, to proclaim God as Trinity is to recognize the ways in which God is loving us into loving, thereby calling us into loving relationship with ourselves, with one another, and with God.

The creating love of God calls us into a life-enhancing relationship with all that God has created and breathed into life. Hence, we are called to guard and protect the sacredness of the earth and all that is therein. This begins with affirming the sacred breath of every single human being, including ourselves. We violate our very sacred breath any time that we use it to violate the sacred breath of another. The saving love of God calls us into relationships that free ourselves and others from the systems, structures, -isms, and ways of being that prevent us or any of God's creation from thriving and growing into the fullness of who and what it was created to be. The advocating love of God beckons us to partner with God in making the truth and justice that is God's heaven real on earth.

The proclamation of God as "holy, blessed, and glorious Trinity, one God," is about nothing less than the ways in which God is loving us into the love dance that is God.

KELLY BROWN DOUGLAS

Almighty and everlasting God, you have given to us your servants grace, by the confession of a true faith, to acknowledge the glory of the eternal Trinity, and in the power of your divine Majesty to worship the Unity: Keep us steadfast in this faith and worship, and bring us at last to see you in your one and eternal glory, O Father; who with the Son and the Holy Spirit live and reign, one God, for ever and ever. Amen.

—The Book of Common Prayer, p.228

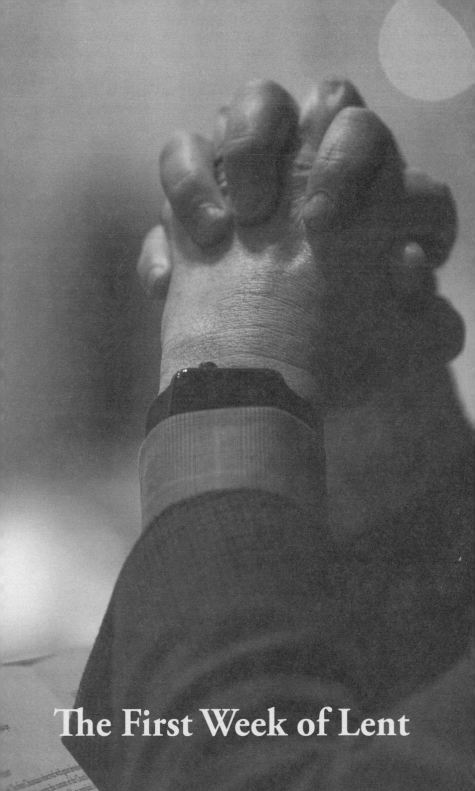

The First Week of Lent

Sunday

Remember not, Lord Christ, our offenses, nor the offenses of our forefathers; neither reward us according to our sins.

Spare us, good Lord, spare thy people, whom thou hast redeemed with thy most precious blood, and by thy mercy preserve us for ever.

Spare us, good Lord.

Sin is a messy business. We all sin. And we all try to go forth and sin no more. And yet, we sin again. It is a vicious cycle. The good news is, for there is always good news in our faith, we can be forgiven, and we can, with God's help, change—if we want to change.

When I was growing up, I always hated the parable of the prodigal son. I thought it was horribly unfair, and I couldn't think of any parents I knew who would throw a party for their child after they had behaved in that way. It just didn't seem realistic to me. As someone who followed the rules to the letter of the law and related to the other son, this story annoyed me to no end, and quite frankly, it didn't even seem true or believable. And then, I became an adult, a parent, a priest, and a teacher, and the parable came to light in a whole new way. I understood the desperate love of a parent for a child who had gone astray. What wouldn't a parent do to bring their child home? What sin would they not forgive? How much singing and rejoicing would there be when the child asks for forgiveness and repents of their sins? Yes, kill the fatted calf. It is time to celebrate, for my child was lost and now they are found.

At the age of 60, I find that the story of the prodigal son is now one of my favorite biblical narratives. I see the parable as analogous to the love God has for each one of us. Like the father in the story, there is no sin that cannot be forgiven by our Lord. This story is God's promise to us that there will be no keeping score of our offenses nor rewarding us according to our misdeeds. God will instead run to meet us, embrace us with a love that has no end, and lead us to the heavenly banquet that awaits us. Thanks be to God. Thanks be to God that this love has no bounds, that there is no sin that can separate us from our Lord.

MELISSA HOLLERITH

Lord, I commit my failures as well as my successes into your hands, and I bring for your healing the people and the situations, the wrongs and the hurts of the past. Give me courage, strength, and generosity to let go and move on, leaving the past behind me and living the present to the full. Lead me always to be positive as I entrust the past to your mercy, the present to your love, and the future to your providence.

—Attributed to Saint Augustine of Hippo, 354–430

Monday

From all evil and wickedness; from sin;
from the crafts and assaults of the devil;
and from everlasting damnation,

Good Lord, deliver us.

Every year, Lent opens with a comfortable reliability. The gospel
appointed for the first Sunday always recounts Jesus's temptation
in the wilderness. Equally as reliable is my own forty-day
struggle with the great tempter. No, this is not a testimony of
battle with the Evil One. It is the same uninspired question I
ask each year: is evil a real thing, an actuality, or the absence of
good? Mark's Gospel describes evil as a being and confidently
names it "the devil."

We generally ignore the devil. For many, the concept is a
dangerous relic. From the serpent in Eden to the apocalyptic
dragon, the names and images of Satan have long been used to
frighten, control, and subjugate. The caricatured rendering of a
red-horned man-beast has dampened our modern reactions even
further. For many, the devil is not a meaningful aspect of their
faith. However, this view diminishes our understanding of evil
and the ways in which we can recognize and reject it.

In early medieval depictions of the temptation of Jesus, the face of the devil is often obscured or hidden. This year as I prepared for Lent, I admitted that my obsession with putting a face on the devil was a distraction born out of childhood fascination. It took me from the difficult work of the forty days. I spent too much time and energy attempting to give life to or put a face on something (or someone) to blame for a world roiled by ecological destruction, devastating pandemics, crushing socioeconomic inequities, and a fraying social fabric.

The story of salvation recounts our best efforts to accept God's love as well as our pitiful failures. Our shortcomings constantly struggle against our intention to lead lives that add to the world's degree of hope and joy as revealed in the gospels. Time and again, we are charmed into pleasant indifference, into an apathetic, narcissistic blandness.

Should we "reclaim" the devil then? Perhaps. I don't know. If we understand the devil as a fantastical character, he/she/it is conveniently dismissed as something only the most literal employ. Cast as "other," the devil has little to do with us. However, there is no outside devil that cannot be found inside us all. We may not know the temptation of being offered inestimable power as Jesus was, but we know the everyday failings of our pride, vanity, and hypocrisy. Likewise, we have all experienced the shameful inclination to envy, judge, and gossip. We have looked away from those in need. We have let anger or apathy direct our actions.

This season, let us begin Lent afresh, committing to the work ahead. As every year, we are invited to take Jesus's same journey into the desert of our souls. The familiar scene looks different: if the devil must have a face, it is mine.

Thanks be to God.

TORRENCE N. THOMAS

Almighty God, whose blessed Son was led by the Spirit to be tempted by Satan: Come quickly to help us who are assaulted by many temptations; and, as you know the weaknesses of each of us, let each one find you mighty to save; through Jesus Christ your Son our Lord, who lives and reigns with you and the Holy Spirit, one God, now and for ever. Amen.

—The Book of Common Prayer, p. 218

Tuesday

From all blindness of heart; from pride, vainglory, and hypocrisy; from envy, hatred, and malice; and from all want of charity,

Good Lord, deliver us.

I say this every Lenten season to anyone who will listen: "I need to give up myself for Lent!" Why me? Because I suffer from blindness of heart—as well as all its adverse side effects (see above). Every year, I experience this blindness of heart as a psychic plaque that's been accumulating around and suffocating my soul since the previous Lent and needs to be scraped— STAT. The pride (my puffed-up sense of self) and vainglory (a terrific word that means I care too much about what others think of me) coat and stain what's best in me. The only cleaning "solution" that works, I've found, is a mix, combining a Lenten confession with a posture of humility.

Henri Frédéric Amiel, a nineteenth-century Swiss moral philosopher, wrote, "There is no respect for others without humility in one's self"—a sentiment rooted in countless Bible verses warning against the sin of pride. Paul admonishes the Corinthians and the Romans for being "puffed up," for thinking too highly of themselves and not enough of others. One could argue that pride is the original sin from which all the others flow—vainglory, hypocrisy, envy, hatred, malice, stinginess. As Jesus warns in Matthew, "All who exalt themselves will be humbled, and all who humble themselves will be exalted" (23:12). Humility is the antidote to pride.

The root of humility is *humus*, which derives from the earth, the ground beneath our feet. It is my hope this Lent that I can ground myself more in Christ Jesus and not in my own untethered vanities as they are blown to and fro. This season is a time to let go of the neediness of my own obsessions and trust that I will feel more contentment when my prayers and hopes are grounded in God and neighbor.

DANA CORSELLO

Gracious and merciful God, help me remove the scales of blindness from my heart. May the sins of my pride and vanities be forgiven and laid to rest in you. Help me relinquish my own ego and refocus my energies in the love and prayers I can offer others in your name. Amen.

Wednesday

From all inordinate and sinful affections;
and from all the deceits of the world,
the flesh, and the devil,

Good Lord, deliver us.

It will surprise no one that this was the last prayer petition to be "claimed" by the contributors for this book! In a weak moment, I told my cathedral colleagues that I would take any petition that went unclaimed. This petition was not top of mind when I made that offer.

There is a natural inclination when considering a challenging prayer petition to focus on the minors. For instance, what exactly does "inordinate" mean in this context? In reality, the discomfort comes from actually knowing what is intended with the petition, despite any attempts to sugarcoat the meaning.

Supreme Court Justice Potter Stewart was famously quoted regarding the characterization of pornography in Jacobellis v. Ohio, 1964. He simply said, "I know it when I see it." There had apparently been a great deal of conversation on how exactly to characterize pornography. Justice Stewart stated the obvious.

In the catechism in the Book of Common Prayer, the seventh of the ten commandments is clear: "To use all our bodily desires as God intended." In the section referencing sin and redemption, sin is described as, "the seeking of our own will instead of the will of God, thus distorting our relationship with God, with other people, and with all creation." It goes on to say that "Sin has power over us because we lose our liberty when our relationship with God is distorted." It is important to remember that in our petition in the Great Litany, we specifically ask for deliverance from sin and deceit and, later in the litany, proclaim thanksgiving that God sent the Messiah to redeem us. As stated in the catechism, "Redemption is the act of God which sets us free from the power of evil, sin, and death" (The Book of Common Prayer, pages 848-849).

One of the most powerful stories of redemption comes in the story of Jesus and the woman caught in adultery (John 7:53—8:11). In this story, the scribes and Pharisees bring a woman caught in adultery before Jesus. They tell Jesus that the law of Moses commands them to stone her, and they ask him for his opinion. Jesus replies, "Let anyone among you who is without sin be the first to throw a stone at her." When they hear Jesus's response, they all go away. Jesus then addresses the woman: "Woman, where are they? Has no one condemned you?" She replies, "No one, sir." And Jesus says, "Neither do I condemn you. Go your way, and from now on do not sin again."

We are in the early stages of our Lenten journey and a time of self-examination and repentance. Hold fast to the redemption that is intended for all with new and contrite hearts. Remember also the words of social justice advocate Bryan Stevenson: "Each of us is more than the worst thing we've ever done."

JAN NAYLOR COPE

*If we say that we have no sin, we deceive ourselves, and the truth
is not in us; but if we confess our sins, God is faithful and just to
forgive us our sins, and to cleanse us from all unrighteousness.*

—The Book of Common Prayer, p. 320

Thursday _____

From all false doctrine, heresy, and schism;
from hardness of heart, and contempt of thy
Word and commandment,

Good Lord, deliver us.

In the Gospel according to Matthew, Jesus says "'You shall love the Lord your God with all your heart, and with all your soul, and with all your mind.' This is the greatest and first commandment. And a second is like it: 'You shall love your neighbor as yourself.' On these two commandments hang all the law and the prophets" (Matthew 22:37-40). If we examine this petition of the Great Litany through the lens of these two commandments, the desire we are expressing to God is that we be delivered from those things that stand in the way of us following God's commandments.

When I read "From all false doctrine, heresy, and schism... Good Lord, deliver us," I think of the ways that these words have been weaponized by some in the pursuit of hatred of their neighbors. For me, the potentially charged nature of these particular words obscures the deeper significance of what these words are pointing toward. False doctrine, heresy, and schism are the result of a disjointed community that is failing to love each other. The antidote, the way of deliverance from such division, is loving our neighbors as ourselves—and we need God's goodness to get us there.

When I read "from hardness of heart, and contempt of thy Word and commandment, Good Lord, deliver us," I think of the call to love God with all our heart. How can we love God if our heart is hardened? How can we love God if we regard God's word with contempt? Lent is the perfect season to take the time to be intentional about opening ourselves up to God, so that we might be able to love God with our full heart and our full self. God already loves us fully and invites all of us into deeper relationship.

This Lent, I invite you to be open and intentional about seeking unity in the church. Only God can deliver us from our pitfalls, but there is work for us to do in our communities, and we can get started today.

JACQUELINE GALVINHILL

Almighty Father, whose blessed Son before his passion prayed for his disciples that they might be one, as you and he are one: Grant that your Church, being bound together in love and obedience to you, may be united in one body by the one Spirit, that the world may believe in him whom you have sent, your Son Jesus Christ our Lord; who lives and reigns with you, in the unity of the Holy Spirit, one God, now and for ever. Amen.

—The Book of Common Prayer, p. 255

Friday

From lightning and tempest;
from earthquake, fire, and flood;
from plague, pestilence, and famine,

Good Lord, deliver us.

At approximately 2 p.m. on August 23, 2011, I heard what
sounded like loud explosions as I sat in my cathedral office.
Shortly thereafter, the floor began to undulate, and my desk
drawers flew open. It wasn't until I heard the cathedral bells ring
discordantly that I realized we were experiencing an earthquake.
The quake, the first major earthquake in the Washington area
in more than 100 years, caused $34 million in damage to the
cathedral, but the true blessing and miracle of the day was that
no one was injured. Several hundred tourists were visiting the
cathedral when the earthquake happened.

What I remember most, more than a decade later, are the people
who immediately reached out to offer support in unexpected
ways. The senior rabbi at the neighboring synagogue offered the
sanctuary for us to hold our Sunday services since they did not
use the space on Sundays. The dean of ChristChurch Cathedral
in New Zealand sent a note of solidarity and a contribution to
help with our restoration—this after their own cathedral had

suffered devastating earthquake damage six months earlier. These are but two examples of the countless number of people who "showed up" in our time of need.

Sadly, news stories of natural disasters are a regular feature across our country and the globe, as are the ravages of plague, pestilence, and famine. Far too many are the result of climate change and our collective failure to be good stewards of that which God has entrusted to us. Just as people reached out to us after the earthquake, so too, we are called to respond to those in need.

People of faith often turn to scripture to consider creation and our role and responsibility as stewards of the earth. We know from Genesis that God called all things into being, including humankind, and pronounced that it was "very good." And then God gave humankind what is translated as dominion over all that was created. Dominion does not mean depleting, defiling, degrading, and destroying. As stewards with God, we have a responsibility to care for and protect God's gift to us —this fragile earth, our island home.

When environmental legend and advocate Wendell Berry spoke at the cathedral, he said that it was our moral obligation to look after this fragile earth. He offered a wonderful twist on the golden rule. Berry put it this way: "Do unto those downstream what you would have those upstream do unto you." We are inextricably interconnected as a global community. May we love God and our neighbors by being good stewards of that which God has entrusted to us and responding generously when our neighbors are in need.

JAN NAYLOR COPE

God of creation, we thank you for all that you have made and called good: Grant that we may rightly serve and conserve the earth and live at peace with all your creatures; through Jesus Christ, the firstborn of all creation, in whom you are reconciling the whole world to yourself. Amen.

—Great Cloud of Witnesses, p. A65

Hear Us, Good Lord

Saturday _____

From all oppression, conspiracy, and rebellion;
from violence, battle, and murder;
and from dying suddenly and unprepared,

Good Lord, deliver us.

We hope that we don't have to deal with the realities of this
prayer. We fight against oppression of all sorts, we cherish our
freedom, and we promote life and peace. We try and try, but we
continue to see again and again the hardships raised in
this prayer:

> *Oppression and discrimination of minorities*
> *The conspiracy to overturn our fundamental rights*
> *The rebellious events of January 6, 2021 in our capital*
> *The consequences of the war in many corners of*
> *the world*
> *The countless premature deaths because of human*
> *conflicts, poverty, pandemic,*
> *and the abuse of creation*

We live in a race against death, and sometimes we feel the
marathon is rigged against us since the beginning. How much
harder can we try? How faster can we go? Sometimes silence is
the only answer.

This prayer of the Great Litany is more current than ever, no matter how hard we try to keep our eyes closed to avoid seeing death, violence, and oppression.

Once and again, we hear Jesus's words from the cross: "Father, forgive them; for they do not know what they are doing" (Luke 23:34). In our own limitation, we do not always know the full consequences of our actions, especially when we are blinded by hate and deception. We try to convince ourselves that there is such a thing as "just war" or a justified violence against "their" evil. But when we try to justify ourselves and our actions, we move further away from God's dream for humanity and creation. That is why we continue praying, crying out to the Good Lord to deliver us from our own human actions of self-destruction and sin.

We pray to God because we believe.
We cry out because we do not give up.
We ask God because there is not deliverance,
if not in our Good Lord.

Yoimel González Hernández

O Jesus, mirror of everlasting love, call to mind the sadness you felt when you looked down from the cross to see a world awash in its sin and the goodness you displayed to the thief to whom you said, "This day you shall be with me in paradise." In memory of the depth of your pity, O my Savior, remember me in the hour of my own death, not weighing my merits but pardoning my offenses. Amen.

—Saint Augustine's Prayer Book, p. 277

The Second Week of Lent

Sunday

By the mystery of thy holy Incarnation;
by thy holy Nativity and submission to the Law;
by thy Baptism, Fasting, and Temptation,

Good Lord, deliver us.

We ask in the Great Litany for deliverance from our many sins and ills. Now we evoke the life of Jesus as we continue to pray for deliverance.

In the second stanza of the hymn, "St. Patrick's Breastplate," often sung on Trinity Sunday, we sing: "I bind this day to me forever, by power of faith, Christ's Incarnation; his baptism in the Jordan river." The rest of the stanza includes Christ's death, resurrection, ascension, and coming again, which are recalled in the next petition in the Great Litany. We don't just remember these events: by faith, we can bind them to ourselves as a breastplate for strength and protection.

We may be familiar with the story of the incarnation, the amazing events surrounding Jesus's birth, his baptism, and his temptation in the wilderness, but how much have we wrestled with them, marveled at them, and learned deeply about how these stories can affect us? Have we bound these lessons to ourselves so that they become a part of us?

We are taught that through his incarnation Jesus became truly human, really one of us, as part of God's plan to reconcile us to God. The truly human Jesus knows our strengths, frailties, and willfulness. Have we bound this to ourselves so that we know, really know, that it is true?

At Jesus's baptism, the Holy Spirit descends upon him, and God proclaims that Jesus is his son, the beloved, with whom God is well pleased (Luke 3:21-22). As we read this story and the service of Holy Baptism in the Book of Common Prayer (starting on page 297), I wonder whether we truly comprehend the power of this action in which we are reborn and "marked as Christ's own forever." Have we bound to ourselves to the immense difference this has made in our lives?

After Jesus's baptism, he prays and fasts in the wilderness. We employ prayer and fasting as a means of drawing closer to God and of recognizing what is superfluous in our lives, but what do we really believe about the efficacy and power of prayer, especially when we feel stuck in the wilderness? How can we bind prayer to ourselves so that it becomes integral to us?

Jesus is tempted by the devil, yet he rebuffs the devil's trickery. Jesus understands temptation's seductive power but shows us that temptation can be overcome. God gives us power to withstand temptation through the Holy Spirit and is always ready to forgive when we sin and repent. Have we bound ourselves to this so that we truly rely on God's power and forgiveness?

I pray that we bind the power in these stories to ourselves.

MICHAEL LEWALLEN

Blessed Lord, who caused all holy Scriptures to be written for our learning: Grant us so to hear them, read, mark, learn, and inwardly digest them, that we may embrace and ever hold fast the blessed hope of everlasting life, which you have given us in our Savior Jesus Christ; who lives and reigns with you and the Holy Spirit, one God, for ever and ever. Amen.

—The Book of Common Prayer, p. 236

Monday

By thine Agony and Bloody Sweat;
by thy Cross and Passion;
by thy precious Death and Burial;
by thy glorious Resurrection and Ascension;
and by the Coming of the Holy Ghost,

Good Lord, deliver us.

In the crypt chapel of Washington National Cathedral, tourists point to a mural and ask why the three Calvary crosses are different shapes. I say something boring about art. My maternal instinct wants to protect these young men, who smile and point, from imagining the scene, from hearing the sound of the nails on the wood.

In the mural, the side crosses are uppercase Ts. It's hard to know what they were in real life. The Romans used several devices: lowercase-T crosses, uppercase-T crosses, X-shaped crosses. Saint Andrew was crucified on an X-shaped cross. Our namesake Saint Peter was crucified upside down, hence the upended crosses that decorate our processional torches. Do our acolytes ever imagine the scene, walking with that image in front of their face, inverted symbol engraved on the wood?

Early Christians thought the cross had a bisecting beam, but they could not bear to draw it, thought of the punishment fresh in their minds. Even now, we don't like to imagine what happened on the cross. It all happened so long ago. I put on my dispassionate finance hat, writing by keeping a distance, describing the technical shape of the wood.

Some say the cross was no more than a pole. The Greek word for cross, *stauros*, can mean stake or pole. An Old English word for pole is *pale*, root of the horrible word impale and the more suburban word palisade, as in palisade fence. There are plenty of palisade fences in town. Walking down a manicured Washington street in springtime, past the embassies and art galleries, I find the crucifixion hard to imagine. It happened so long ago. All I can hear are the sounds of an army of landscapers behind the big fences, young men working, working, clipping too close and hitting the wood.

But these ordinary fences bring the horror home. For in the crypt chapel, across from the mural, lie the remains of Matthew Wayne Shepard, a gay student who attended the University of Wyoming. He was beaten, tortured, and left to die on a buck-rail fence. That's a fence with X-shaped end posts spaced six feet apart, rails balanced between them. He hung on that fence for 18 hours, a young man, breathing, breathing, clinging to life through the feel of the wood.

Good Lord. Deliver us.

ELIZABETH JOHNS

O Lord who makes all things new, we thank you for what you have done for us. Bring us with all your followers to be with you in your new creation, where we all can be healed and whole again. Amen.

Hear Us, Good Lord

Tuesday

In all time of our tribulation;
in all time of our prosperity;
in the hour of death,
and in the day of judgment,

Good Lord, deliver us.

"I can't believe it's over," my mother said to me, tears streaming down our faces, as she prepared to enroll in hospice care. Only 62, with a loving marriage, a zest for travel, and two young grandchildren she adored, she never imagined her life would be coming to an end so abruptly or her days so filled with physical and spiritual pain. She was heartbroken. We all were.

In the midst of her suffering and our sadness, family and friends came together to create a web of caring and tenderness that became a prayer, a living reflection of God's love and grace. We shared memories and offered words of gratitude—and apology. Farewells were written and spoken. There were plenty of tears, along with a good bit of laughter.

As the end neared, Mom drifted in and out of lucidity for several days. My father, brother, and I were gathered near when she spoke words we never expected to hear, "I'm ready, I'm ready, I'm ready." Her eyes, half closed for the past few days, opened wide in awe and wonder as a gentle smile came upon her face. In that moment, I felt God's presence in a way I had never experienced or even imagined, bearing witness as God delivered her safely into the life beyond this life.

In the years since my mother's death, I saw God at work among the dying many times over. As a hospice volunteer, I entered the lives of hundreds of people through encounters as brief as delivering a meal tray or changing a diaper and more intimate ones that developed into relationships lasting weeks and months.

I witnessed time and again—in my own and others' experiences—that at certain moments, God calls us to walk alongside a dying person. They may be someone very close to us or they may be a distant friend or acquaintance. If we answer God's call by turning toward the one who is dying, by offering open ears and open hearts, we create possibilities for healing—theirs and ours.

Each time I had the privilege to be beside someone at the moment of death, I was overcome by the presence of the Holy Spirt. I found, as I did with my mother, that the very end is often quite peaceful; it's the weeks, days, and hours before that are most often filled with struggle. Few people wish to travel that territory alone.

Just as we call on God to deliver us at the hour of death, so too does God call on us, as his hands and feet in this world, to come beside others as they prepare to cross the threshold into the arms of mercy.

G. Scott Sanders

*Into your hands, O merciful Savior, we commend your servant.
Acknowledge, we humbly beseech you, a sheep of your own fold, a
lamb of your own flock, a sinner of your own redeeming. Receive
her into the arms of your mercy, into the blessed rest of everlasting
peace, and into the glorious company of the saints in light.* Amen.

—The Book of Common Prayer, p. 465

Wednesday

We sinners do beseech thee to hear us,
   O Lord God;
and that it may please thee to rule
and govern thy holy Church Universal
   in the right way,

We beseech thee to hear us, good Lord.

As we continue our Lenten journey and await the radiant joy of Easter in about thirty days' time, we humbly ask God to hear us, to listen to us as we engage in self-reflection and focus on the essential: what is core to our being? What is profoundly important? God is listening. Are we?

Three years ago this week, our world was put on pause. Suddenly and unexpectedly, we found ourselves grappling with an unknown and frightening virus and retreated to our homes. We had no idea that a two-week closure of our offices and schools would become two years and beyond of a global "new normal" or that the concept of complete eradication would evolve into continued caution and vigilance.

So much changed, but, as my colleague, the Rev. Canon Rosemarie Logan Duncan, often says, "Sunday comes." Despite the horrors described on the nightly news, the sun rose every morning and set a bit later each evening. Snowdrops poked through in the shade garden behind the nave. Spring, and Easter, would come. Unmoored from our usual routines and unsure of when we could return to in-person worship, the remaining days of Lent seemed to stretch unendingly before us. When could we safely return to the cathedral? March 25? May 15? No one was certain.

As commutes halted and non-essential businesses were shuttered, many noticed that the city of Washington was quiet, very quiet. The ominous sound of sirens was not accompanied by the usual honking to wade through traffic. Through our worry, we could now hear the birds. Their melodious, joyful song seemed somehow elevated from what we remembered of pre-pandemic springs—more noticeable, more worthy of our collective attention. As a community, we engaged in active listening to these birdsongs and compared notes from our respective homes on Twitter (tweeting about tweeting!). A study reported in the journal *Science* confirmed that birds in urban areas quickly adapted to the quiet, "producing higher performance songs at lower amplitudes, effectively maximizing communication distance and salience."

As we ask God to listen to us, we, too, must listen and trust God to lead us in the way we should be led. During Lent, we pare things down so that our faith can lift us up. With less noise, we truly hear the word of God, just as we experienced the unique birdsongs of our first pandemic spring.

Listen well and more deeply in the coming weeks. Consider the joy that is to come.

KATHERINE M. PRENDERGAST

Then shall all the trees of the wood shout for joy before the LORD when he comes, when he comes to judge the earth. He will judge the world with righteousness and the peoples with his truth.

—Psalm 96:12-13

Thursday

That it may please thee to illumine
all bishops, priests, and deacons,
with true knowledge and understanding of thy Word;
and that both by their preaching and living,
they may set it forth, and show it accordingly,

We beseech thee to hear us, good Lord.

The Falmouth Road Race starts in the peninsular hamlet
of Woods Hole and traces seven miles of rolling Cape Cod
coastline before plummeting to the finish along Grand Avenue.
It's a great race—ocean views, competitive field, spectators
replete with orange slices, and well-placed sprinklers. Apart from
the suffocating heat and humidity that plague the race every five
years or so, the only downside is that getting to the start requires
everyone's least favorite form of transportation: a bus.

A few years ago, three friends cheered me on at the finish.
We split into pairs and decided to meet up at the beach. My
best friend, Leslie, pulled up directions to my car, which was
parked at the bus-loading area (that I thought was nearby), and
discovered that it was three and a half miles away. Her phone
battery was nearly dead; I was carrying only my car key and the
complimentary race tote bag.

"Ok, you remember these streets: Harbor, Robbins, Scranton. We need to turn left," she said.

We walked straight for three or four blocks. "Harbor!" We turned left. In another three or four blocks, Leslie turned right. "I thought we were looking for a left on Robbins?" I asked.

"We are. But first we need to turn right on Heights."

"Oh, well you didn't say that."

"I know. We have to go left-right three times to get back to the car. You're remembering all the streets where we have to turn left. I'm remembering all the streets where we have to turn right. And we're alternating."

There are rare occasions for us to actually see the human brain at work, to bear stunning witness to another person's mind operating on a level far more complex than our own. Yet, day after day, the clergy I have come to know as friends and colleagues compel the same awe that I felt standing on the corner of Harbor Avenue and Falmouth Heights Road. In the biggest celebration among family or the smallest interaction with a stranger, their awareness of the moment is surpassed only by the depth of their compassion, and they combine the two by some secret recipe, some seeming magic.

As a person of faith, I seek this magic in the same places but emerge having gleaned something different. If to read the words on the page is to be a believer, then to live the spaces between the words—and the words unwritten—is to be called. The ordained hear a voice that I do not; it teaches them how to solve problems with no solutions and chart paths with no maps. They seem to know how to make yellow from a palette of only blue and red, then wrap their hands around mine and lead the brush gently across the canvas. When the painting is done, they compliment how beautiful the work is, and, at once, I feel both blessed and unworthy to receive this gift that I do not possess myself and can only know through their presence.

So, what can I do aside from stare at the canvas in grateful marvel? I plead for the Lord to protect their special gifts, that I and others might find refuge in them during times of need. May we all beseech the Lord to shine brightly upon them, that the cast of their light might help guide our way. And may we delight in their understanding of the Word, knowing it will in Deed shape us forever.

GABRIELLE McKENZIE

Almighty God, the giver of all good gifts, in your divine providence you have appointed various orders in your Church: Give your grace, we humbly pray, to all who are called to any office and ministry for your people; and so fill them with the truth of your doctrine and clothe them with holiness of life, that they may faithfully serve before you, to the glory of your great Name and for the benefit of your holy Church; through Jesus Christ our Lord, who lives and reigns with you, in the unity of the Holy Spirit, one God, now and for ever. Amen.

—The Book of Common Prayer, p. 256

Friday

That it may please thee to bless
and keep all thy people,

We beseech thee to hear us, good Lord.

"May I bless you?" It was a busier than usual Tuesday evening at
the cathedral. As I dashed from the Centering Prayer gathering
in the crypt to check in with the labyrinth volunteers in the
nave, I was mentally crossing off the tasks on my to-do list when
I heard someone call my name. I was stopped by a friend for
a quick hug and hello, but as I cut our conversation short and
made my excuses to leave, she grabbed my hand and asked the
question, "May I bless you?"

One aspect of the Celtic Christian tradition that deeply
resonates with my spiritual DNA is the practice of blessing.
In the land of my ancestors, there are blessings for all the
rhythms and responsibilities of daily life, from waking up in the
morning to blessing one's household and neighbors at night,
and everything in between. The threshold of each new hour or
activity is an opportunity to pause for prayer, to bless the next
step in our day or in the day of a fellow pilgrim we encounter.
The blessing doesn't have to be eloquent or elaborate, just a
simple act or a few words as a reminder that God is present in

whatever we are doing or experiencing, be it lighting a candle before booting up our laptop to start the workday, saying grace at mealtimes, or bidding a visitor farewell with a goodbye and the words, God be with you.

Never one to turn down a blessing, I bent down as my friend marked my forehead with the sign of the cross. She whispered the familiar words from the book of Numbers, "The Lord bless you and keep you. The Lord make his face to shine upon you and be gracious to you. The Lord lift up his countenance upon you and give you peace." In that moment, my whole being sighed into the awareness that, under the hurrying and scurrying of my body and mind, the peace of the Holy One was indeed with me.

God does bless us and is pleased, dare I say delighted, to do so; but at times we need to reach out a hand, hear another voice to be reminded that the Lord blesses and keeps us, all of us.

TERRI LYNN SIMPSON

God, bless to me this day.
God, bless to me this night.
Bless, O Bless, Thou God of grace,
Each day and hour of my life;
Bless, O bless, Thou God of grace,
Each day and hour of my life.

—Traditional Scottish prayer
from *Carmina Gadelica*
by Alexander Carmichael

Saturday

That it may please thee to send forth
laborers into thy harvest,
and to draw all mankind into thy kingdom,

We beseech thee to hear us, good Lord.

In Luke, chapter 10, and in Matthew, chapter 9, we hear our Lord say, "The harvest is plentiful, but the laborers are few." Today, Jesus Christ is still the Lord of the harvest, and he is still calling folks to join him in the work, to draw people to him. So, what does that look like for us?

Saint Teresa of Avila put it this way: "Christ has no body now on earth but yours, no hands but yours, no feet but yours, yours are the eyes through which Christ's compassion is to look out to the earth, yours are the feet by which he is to go about doing good and yours are the hands by which he is to bless us now."

So, what is Jesus's big strategic plan for growing the kingdom on earth? He's counting on us, on our hands and feet working to spread the good news. So, how can we be laborers? Where is the harvest?

Jesus once again uses an agriculture metaphor to tell us that there is a ripe harvest of lost people, people who are spiritually hungry. They are hungry not necessarily for food but to know about God. And they want to be shepherded, led, to this knowledge. However, many of us don't always point them toward Jesus, and we aren't always comfortable sharing the good news. But this needs to change. If our lives have been transformed because of the good news of Jesus Christ, we must not shy away from sharing this truth. Sometimes the message of the salvation gospel is shared through words but more often than not, the message is shared by our actions. When we feed the hungry, when we care for the infirmed, when we welcome the stranger, we are joining Christ in his work.

May we all labor on in Jesus's name, may we tend to the harvest in his name's sake, for the harvest is plentiful and the laborers are few.

MELISSA HOLLERITH

Help us, Lord, to remember your call to us: Come labor on. Who dares stand idle on the harvest plain, while all around us waves the golden grain? And to each servant does the Master say, "Go work today." Amen.

—Adapted from "Come, Labor On," *The Hymnal 1982*,
words by Jane Laurie Borthwick

The Second Week of Lent

The Third Week of Lent

Sunday

That it may please thee to give to all people increase of grace to hear and receive thy Word, and to bring forth the fruits of the Spirit,

We beseech thee to hear us, good Lord.

I invite you, therefore, in the name of the Church, to the observance of a holy Lent, by self-examination and repentance; by prayer, fasting, and self-denial; and by reading and meditating on God's holy Word.

—The Book of Common Prayer, p. 265

Responding to this invitation requires our investment of time and intention so that we may hear and receive God's word more fully. Making time to read scripture with intention means allowing ourselves to be open to new ways of understanding. Many of us have read the Bible multiple times and are particularly familiar with and drawn to certain texts. Often, this may lead us to hastily read the day's lessons and miss the opportunity to hear something differently in the text or find new meaning. At different points in our lives, scripture can bring new insights and learnings to deepen our faith and our relationship with God.

Meditating on scripture requires focus and quietness. Meditation is not only about remembering history but also engaging God in our own personal stories. It means focusing our attention on God's message not just to our ancestors in faith but to us in our own lives today. Truly the word of God is living and active, not locked in the past to a particular place and time. For God's word then to be living and active in us and in the world means that we must allow ourselves to be transformed by it.

One of my favorite collects tells us that all scriptures are meant for our learning so we should hear them, read, mark, learn, and inwardly digest them. I have always been struck by the odd phrase of inwardly digest. I have come to understand that we are invited to engage in an ongoing process of reading and ingesting, literally taking in scripture as nourishment for our souls and bodies. The good news is that we are not left to our own devices with this process of hearing and receiving, of reading and meditating. The catechism reminds us that "we understand the meaning of the Bible by the help of the Holy Spirit" (The Book of Common Prayer, p. 853-54).

Our petition today reminds us that God's grace—that favor toward us, unearned and undeserved—has the power to enlighten our minds, stir our hearts, and strengthen our wills so that we may hear and receive God's word. May we hold this truth in our hearts during this season of Lent and every day of our lives.

ROSEMARIE LOGAN DUNCAN

Blessed Lord, who caused all holy Scriptures to be written for our learning: Grant us so to hear them, read, mark, learn, and inwardly digest them, that we may embrace and ever hold fast the blessed hope of everlasting life, which you have given us in our Savior Jesus Christ; who lives and reigns with you and the Holy Spirit, one God, for ever and ever. Amen.

—The Book of Common Prayer, p. 236

Monday

That it may please thee to bring
into the way of truth
all such as have erred, or that are deceived,

We beseech thee to hear us, good Lord.

I love the meditative quality of the Great Litany. I find it
allows me to still my thoughts and place myself in the Lord's
presence, lulled by the rhythm of the recitation, the power of
the language, the familiarity of the refrain.

But as I prepared this meditation and focused not on the effect
of its words but on their meaning, I was struck by how much we
ask of the Lord.

In the deprecations at the litany's beginning, we seek delivery
from the evils of the world that we cannot control (e.g.,
earthquake, fire and flood) and from even more that we can—or
should—control (e.g., sinful affections, false doctrine, hardness
of heart, conspiracy, violence, oppressions).

And in the prayers of intercession of which today's reading is
a part, we again ask much. Our entreaties assume the Lord's
abiding love, grace, and forgiveness.

Today's reading raises up the gift of forgiveness and the accompanying promise of redemption. Reflecting on this reading, my mind goes immediately to myself and the many ways I have erred just in recent days. I reflect on one-off failings: the stray comment to a colleague that was too sharp; the thoughtless way I engaged another without regard to their personal history; my failure to fulfill a promise to someone in need. I think about my even larger errs: the way I have allowed my to-do list and overscheduled days to be an excuse for not finding and following the Lord; how I have allowed myself to be cosseted by the privileged world in which I live, without appropriate regard for others' needs; how I have allowed pride and ambition to cloud my judgment.

As I look around me in our increasingly troubled world, I see so many others struggling on their own paths. Deceived by inaccurate and misleading information, by their own fears or baser instincts, by the promise of power or material wealth, neighbors are turning against each other, using everything from painful words to senseless violence to cause deep pain.

But the message of today's section of the litany—its reference to the promise and the invitation of our Lord's resurrection—helps me battle back the dark, disturbing implications of these observations. The fact that despite our human failings, some of them extreme, the Lord may still be pleased to welcome us into the way of truth offers me a deep and abiding comfort.

LAURALYNN LEE

Almighty God, our heavenly Father: we have sinned against, through our own fault, in thought, and word, and deed, and in what we have left undone. For the sake of your Son our Lord Jesus Christ, forgive us all our offenses; and grant that we may serve you in newness of life, to the glory of your Name. Amen.

—The Book of Common Prayer, p. 127

Tuesday

That it may please thee to give us
a heart to love and fear thee,
and diligently to live after thy commandments,

We beseech thee to hear us, good Lord.

I dream of a heart to love God better—to love God so much that this love spills over into love of neighbor so that I might follow the two greatest commandments. Some days I ache for a heart so full of love for God that my fears of failure, vulnerability, loneliness, and not-enough-ness are washed away.

But how am I to understand a heart to fear God? My beloved, an Episcopal priest, tells the story of an elderly woman she visited weekly for months. Despite her pain and exhaustion, this woman was afraid to die because as a child, she had been told that God would send her to eternal damnation because of some inconsequential mistake. This fear knit itself into her faith and her body so deeply that both, for a time, refused her a peaceful death. Many of us have been told stories of a God who punishes, casts out, condemns. Some of us, myself included, have struggled, again and again, to uproot these stories. This fear is the antithesis of the God I know.

In case you, too, find yourself digging out of old stories, I offer this. First, and somewhat helpful, is the reminder that the word fear can be read as *awe*—a visceral and spiritual glimpse of the divine. Although the leap to awe requires some mental gymnastics, it creates new possibilities.

What if this petition were an invitation to be honest with myself about the places I do fear God? There are, certainly, the false stories—that human mistakes or desires make me deserving of punishment. But in addition, there is fear that prevents me from simply being honest. This fear encourages me to avoid difficult conversations, to keep quiet, to say "yes" when I would rather say "no." Perhaps your fears are different, but I think we all have them.

Every week, at the end of their visit, my beloved would remind her parishioner: "You are loved, beyond measure, by God who will welcome you home." Eventually, this woman was able to know, truly, that God loved her. It was only after she was honest about her fear that love could cast it out. So too, I hope, it will be with me, that as I am honest about my fears, they will be cast out through love. And with this heart of love for God, for my neighbor, for the people with whom I journey, I will follow the commandments.

MICHELLE DIBBLEE

Lord, let me never presume on your mercy, forget my mortal limitations, or take your goodness for granted. Before the great and unfathomable wonder that is creation, let me stand in silence and awe of its creator, and as I rejoice in your love, let me bear in mind your healing, yet piercing, judgment. Amen.

—Saint Augustine's Prayer Book, p. 73

Wednesday

That it may please thee so to rule the hearts
of thy servants, the President of the United States
(or of this nation), and all others in authority,
that they may do justice, and love mercy,
and walk in the ways of truth,

We beseech thee to hear us, good Lord.

Faith leaders have always cared about politics. The actions
of "all others in authority" are important and an appropriate
subject for our supplications to God because those in authority
affect the lives of countless others —especially the weak, poor,
vulnerable, and mentally and physically challenged. Of those to
whom great authority is given, much will be required, says the
tradition. But how do we pray for them?

Popular cable news host Rachel Maddow has a favorite warning
she issues to viewers on a regular basis: "Don't pay attention to
what they say; pay attention to what they do."

She is referring to politicians, of course. Many of those "in
authority" are politicians, having been given that authority

by voters and charged with good governance of the people in service to the common good. Many of those running for public office will say nearly anything to be elected. And once in office, they will say nearly anything to keep the favor of those who elected them. The problem is not in what they say but in their willingness and commitment to doing what they say and acting in accord with what they have promised. We all know that there is a great gap between what gets said and what gets done. Politicians (good ones and bad) all hope we won't notice that gap.

The Episcopal Church's current Book of Common Prayer contains a mistake: in the prayer book's catechism, under the section on the Old Covenant, the catechist is asked "What response did God require from the chosen people?" The answer: "God required the chosen people to be faithful; to love justice, to do mercy, and to walk humbly with their God."

The answer, obviously meaning to quote the Book of the Prophet Micah 6:8, pulls a switcheroo on us: Instead of loving justice and doing mercy, as the catechism states, Micah actually commands us "to *do* justice, and to *love* kindness, and to walk humbly with your God." I'm guessing this mistake has largely gone unnoticed, because to be honest, it is far easier to love justice than to do justice. Talk is easy, and we can love justice all the livelong day! What God requires of us, however, is much, much harder: to actually *do* justice, which requires strength, perseverance, and above all, courage.

When we pray for those in authority (including and especially the president of our nation), the Great Litany rightly prays that our leaders will do justice and love mercy. While we're at it, perhaps this Lent we should look in a mirror and pray that we, ourselves, might do justice, not merely brag about how much we admire it.

GENE ROBINSON

O God, ruler of our souls, give to our leaders the desire to do justice, not merely give lip service to it. Build in me the integrity and courage to live according to your word, that my life—and not just my words—might reflect your love for every human being. Amen.

Thursday

That it may please thee to make wars
to cease in all the world;
to give to all nations unity, peace, and concord;
and to bestow freedom upon all peoples,

We beseech thee to hear us, good Lord.

"Love thy neighbor as thyself" is something most of us have heard at some point. I remember hearing it the most when I was growing up, and teachers taught us about playing nice with each other and getting along with schoolmates. As an adult, I hear the phrase less often. I still take the meaning to heart, but because I don't hear the words as often, I don't take as much time to reflect on my actions and their impact on others.

Just because we are adults does not mean we are done growing up. I believe that no matter how old or wise we are, we are always still growing up. There is always something new to learn; there are always opportunities to open our minds. Sometimes, we even must relearn things we were taught in earlier years. When I went out into the world as a young adult, I had to relearn what it meant to "love thy neighbor as thyself," and I still have times when I'm faced with a situation where I have to relearn it again.

This petition beseeches God to bring harmony to earth. We pray for freedom for all people and an end to wars and conflicts. While these words show our intent to help, our actions must speak louder. We must relearn to love our neighbors as ourselves. If our collective actions speak louder than our voices as we pray this litany, then we could bring peace to earth.

This Lenten season, we should take time to think about our actions and the effect they have on the world. At the end of each Sunday when we hear the words, "Walk in love as Christ loved us," we should take them into our hearts, and with each step into the world, walk with the love of God in our hearts and the intention to spread God's love with our neighbors.

MEGAN A. BLELLOCH

We humbly beseech thee, O Father, mercifully to look upon our infirmities; and, for the glory of thy Name, turn from us all those evils that we most justly have deserved; and grant that in all our troubles we may put our whole trust and confidence in thy mercy, and evermore serve thee in holiness and pureness of living, to thy honor and glory; through our only Mediator and Advocate, Jesus Christ our Lord. Amen.

—The Book of Common Prayer, p. 155

Hear Us, Good Lord

Friday

That it may please thee to show thy pity
upon all prisoners and captives,
the homeless and the hungry,
and all who are desolate and oppressed,

We beseech thee to hear us, good Lord.

This petition immediately evoked a flashback to an experience
I had in 2018. In July of that year, the Episcopal Church was
gathered in Austin, Texas for the triennial General Convention.
On Sunday, some 1,000 plus of us boarded 19 buses and
traveled about 30 miles outside of Austin for a public witness at
a detention center. At the time, it held more than 500 women
who had been separated from their families at the southern
border and, in some cases, from their children, and were seeking
asylum. The detention center looked like a prison—because it
had been. It was awful, with a few small windows and fencing
all around.

To my surprise, we didn't stop at the detention center. We kept
driving. Finally, the buses pulled over, and we all poured out of
the buses. I could see that there was a roped off platform area,
and I realized it was where we were granted a permit to gather
and assemble. We held our signs saying that the Episcopal
Church cares, that we love you, that you're not alone, and we
began to chant and sing.

The women in the center were so far away that I wasn't sure they could see or hear us, and I began to get discouraged. After a while, I saw some people in our group start to move away from the crowd, and my beloved sister in Christ and friend Rose Duncan and I peeled off and went rogue. We walked back to the front of the detention center and got as close as we could and started to chant, "You are loved. You are not alone. You are not forgotten." Suddenly, we could see in those tiny windows that women were waving white pieces of paper. They saw us, and we saw them! We began to chant even louder. "No están solas! You are not alone!" *We see you. We love you. You are not forgotten.* The women continued to wave. We stayed there until we were asked by the authorities to leave and get back on our buses.

We were later told that one of the women in the center was able to make a phone call, and she reported that the women had been glued to their windows the whole time: from when the first bus arrived until the last bus left, and they were crying because they could see that they were not forgotten, that we were with them, that they were not alone.

This experience haunts me to this day, as well it should. Our petition for today asks us to show pity, but we must also act to build the kingdom of God where all receive equal justice and equal opportunity, and as the prayer for today beseeches, that all may enjoy a fair portion of the riches of this land.

JAN NAYLOR COPE

Hear Us, Good Lord

Look with pity, O heavenly Father, upon the people in this land who live with injustice, terror, disease, and death as their constant companions. Have mercy upon us. Help us to eliminate our cruelty to these our neighbors. Strengthen those who spend their lives establishing equal protection of the law and equal opportunities for all. And grant that every one of us may enjoy a fair portion of the riches of this land; through Jesus Christ our Lord. Amen.

—The Book of Common Prayer, p. 826

Saturday

That it may please thee to give
and preserve to our use
the bountiful fruits of the earth,
so that in due time all may enjoy them,

We beseech thee to hear us, good Lord.

From the very beginning of the creation story, we find an inseparable connection between the earth that God created and humankind made of the earth in the image of God. We find the complete interdependence of creation, with humankind designed to relate to God, one another, and the rest of the created order. On the sixth day, God created living creatures of every kind before creating humankind, and we are told that God saw everything that he had made, and indeed, it was very good. All of creation is a reflection of God's beauty and goodness, glory, and very being.

God gave the care of this earth to our first parents, and that sacred responsibility has passed into our hands. We are charged with tilling and keeping the earth, the dirt, from which we are made and to which we will return at our death. While we affirm that God-given authority to steward the earth, we cannot consider it a license to abuse the creation of which we are a part.

One of the most fundamental acts we are called to do then is to care for God's creation.

Throughout the biblical narrative, God's care for all of creation is repeatedly expressed. Noah is commanded not only to save his household but also to gather pairs of every living creature. God's covenant is with all creation: humankind and every living creature on earth. The psalms also capture God's creative nature and God's desire for the earth's preservation and care as the creator and sustainer of all life. In Paul's letter to the Colossians, we hear that the good news we are called to proclaim includes the promise that Jesus Christ came to redeem all creation.

Several years ago, General Convention explored trial use of creation care language in the Baptismal Covenant, with the addition of a sixth question, "Will you cherish the wondrous works of God, and protect the beauty and integrity of all creation?" Along with an option to expand the fifth baptismal vow of justice to include the dignity of the earth, this addition would have addressed our responsibility as baptized Christians to care for creation. While the resolution never received a final floor vote, it calls us to remember the charge given at creation by God and provides a strong reminder that our failure to serve as faithful caretakers of creation has local and global consequences. Our care for creation reflects our love of one another as an act of discipleship. So that all may enjoy the resources of the earth, let us remember this Lent our duty to conserve and renew all creation.

ROSEMARIE LOGAN DUNCAN

Bountiful Creator, you open your hand to satisfy the needs of every living creature: Make us always thankful for your loving providence, and grant that we, remembering the account we must one day give, may be faithful stewards of your abundance, for the benefit of the whole creation; through Jesus Christ our Lord, through whom all things were made, and who lives and reigns with you and the Holy Spirit, one God, for ever and ever. Amen.

—Great Cloud of Witnesses, p. A63

The Fourth Week of Lent

Sunday

That it may please thee to inspire us,
in our several callings,
to do the work which thou givest us to
do with singleness of heart as thy servants,
and for the common good,

We beseech thee to hear us, good Lord.

Each one of us, by virtue of our baptism, is called to ministry.
As we are all uniquely created children of God, so too our call
to ministry is unique for each of us. God plants on our hearts
the stirrings of something that makes us come alive and find
meaning and purpose in this world. In the church context,
we often use the word vocation to describe this idea, though
too often we unhelpfully limit the use of the term to ordained
ministry. That is far too narrow an understanding of the
concept, for all of us have a vocation—a calling, to get in touch
with the root of this word, which comes from the Latin word
meaning "to call" (*vocare*).

It can be a daunting task to consider what we feel God is calling
us to do with the one precious gift that is our life. It requires a
process of slow and attentive listening for that voice that speaks
in the depths of our souls. We do well to follow the wisdom of

the psalmist who says, "for God alone my soul in silence waits" (Psalm 62:1). We must listen for God's voice in such moments of silence, but we must also learn to listen to our lives—to look to the circumstances of our lives as sources of wisdom and insight, indeed as a primary way in which God speaks to us. Our skills and talents, our interests and passions, those things that bring us joy, a sense of fulfillment, or a deep sense of satisfaction—all these tell us much about what it is we are called to do.

In the Christian context, vocation must also, in some way, connect to service of God and others. We can be assured that something is a genuine vocation, a calling from God, when it both connects with the deepest longings of our hearts and flows outward in some form of service beyond ourselves.

We pray not only for the wisdom to perceive and understand our own sense of vocation but also for the courage and strength to live it out with "singleness of heart...and for the common good." Living out our vocation, to be in touch with the way God created us to live, can be deeply satisfying but also demanding and difficult work. We do not travel the journey alone, though, and we trust that the one who placed that call on our hearts will indeed give us the grace and power to do it.

PATRICK KEYSER

Almighty and everlasting God, by whose Spirit the whole body of your faithful people is governed and sanctified: Receive our supplications and prayers, which we offer before you for all members of your holy Church, that in their vocation and ministry they may truly and devoutly serve you; through our Lord and Savior Jesus Christ, who lives and reigns with you, in the unity of the Holy Spirit, one God, now and for ever. Amen.

—The Book of Common Prayer, p. 256-257

Hear Us, Good Lord

Monday _____

That it may please thee to preserve all
who are in danger by reason of their labor
or their travel,

We beseech thee to hear us, good Lord.

To ponder these words is to see a thousand faces of those in
danger.

Faces like those of 72-year-old Liubov, paralyzed by a stroke,
as she travels in the back of an ambulance over war-torn
Ukrainian roads, and that of her driver, Sasha, who has spent
weeks searching for the elderly and isolated amidst deserted and
shell-shocked towns and villages in hopes of getting them to
relative safety.

Faces like Yossell, a 9-year-old boy who made his way alone,
mostly on foot, from Honduras to the United States, in hopes
of connecting with his grandfather in North Carolina, or Yusef,
who was disowned by his family at age 17 for being gay and
lived for two years as a refugee in Kenya, enduring assaults and
constantly fearing for his life, before making his way to safety.

To offer these words in prayer from the security of my own home, is to pray, at least for now, for the other. For Liubov and Sasha, Yossel and Yusef, and the millions more whose journeys put them in harm's way. I can never fully imagine their trauma. Yet, no matter how far or distant their struggles, I can begin to imagine their fear and heartache, their longing for comfort and rest. While their circumstances are far removed from my own, their humanity is not.

Each of these travelers is a child of God. They too want to be alive and well. They seek protection from the bone-chilling cold of the mountains and the raging heat of the desert, just as I would. Their stomachs feel the same deep pangs of hunger after days without food; their hearts yearn for a kind gesture from a stranger and the reassuring embrace of a loved one.

As we petition God to protect them, we know that too often their journeys are long and circuitous. While Liubov or Sasha, Yossel or Yusef may arrive safely at their next destination, they may well be displaced from their homelands or separated from their families for months, years, or even a lifetime.

We pray to God to become their companion over the days and across the miles in the hope that they will find their way home or arrive at a new home that brings with it the promise and possibility of a new beginning.

G. Scott Sanders

Merciful and loving God, walk beside those who travel this day in search of safety and a new life. Cover them with your loving care and shelter them from harm, bring them through the storms of war and the anguish of oppression, reunite them with their loved ones when possible, and nourish their bodies and souls, that they may find in you the courage to hope and the strength to persevere. Amen.

Tuesday

That it may please thee to preserve,
and provide for, all women in childbirth,
young children and orphans, the widowed,
and all whose homes are broken or torn by strife,

We beseech thee to hear us, good Lord.

When I meditate on this petition, I think of the Beatitudes Jesus offers in Matthew's Gospel: "Blessed are the poor in spirit, for theirs is the kingdom of heaven...Blessed are those who mourn, for they will be comforted...Blessed are the meek, for they will inherit the earth...Blessed are the pure in heart, for they will see God. Blessed are those who are persecuted for righteousness' sake, for theirs is the kingdom of heaven" (5:3-10). *Jesus, please,* I think, *bless the women of child-bearing age, the children, the orphans, the widows whose homes are under siege by war—these most vulnerable souls among us. Bless and protect them. Preserve them with hope and a sense of the future, always.*

I think, too, of what the poet Khalil Gibran wrote in *The Prophet*. "Your children are not your children. They are the sons and daughters of Life's longing for itself. They come through you but not from you. And though they are with you, they belong not to you." This comforting sentiment reminds me that our children, our beloveds, belong to their creator. We are but stewards, and only for a time. We must trust that they and the most vulnerable are always held in the tight embrace of God's loving, merciful, and protective arms and that their suffering is immersed in the mysterious, healing presence of God, if not in my lifetime, then in theirs.

DANA CORSELLO

You know my heart, Lord, that all you have given me, I intend to spend on them and to use it all in their service and yours. O Lord God, keep watch over them day and night. Tenderly spread your wings to protect them, stretch forth your right hand to bless them. Pour into their hearts your Holy Spirit to abide with them, to refresh them, to give them hope, to make them humble before you, and to kindle in them the fire of your love. May the Holy Spirit, the comforter, protect them in temptation and be their strength in all the trials and tribulations of this life. Amen.

—Saint Augustine's Prayer Book, p. 82

Wednesday

That it may please thee to visit the lonely;
to strengthen all who suffer in mind, body,
and spirit; and to comfort with thy presence
those who are failing and infirm,

We beseech thee to hear us, good Lord.

When we wake in the morning, it is reasonable to conclude that our thoughts are generally focused on the activities that will affect our lives directly. Our thoughts are often drawn to the tasks that will be pleasing to us and provide a degree of personal benefit. Before our feet hit the floor, our thoughts shape the day. How often do we wake or start our days thinking of others with a level of concern and regard that our actions cannot help but follow?

Our focus on this part of the litany calls us to consider our neighbors who are in need. These are our neighbors who are lonely, suffering in mind, body, spirit, and those who are failing and infirmed. Our prayer and petition are that they might be comforted by God's presence. I am appreciative of the thoughts that are raised by this petition but also challenged when I consider how God's presence is brought to those in need.

As disciples of Jesus Christ and servants who are sent out to bring good news, we must never forget that the comfort of God's presence is present with those in need not because we have sent God but present because God has sent us. The noted theologian Henri Nouwen wrote about this ministry of presence in his book, *¡Gracias! A Latin American Journal*:

> More and more, the desire grows in me simply to walk around, greet people, enter their homes, sit on their doorsteps, play ball, throw water, and be known as someone who wants to live with them. It is a privilege to have the time to practice this simple ministry of presence. Still, it is not as simple as it seems. My own desire to be useful, to do something significant, or to be part of some impressive project is so strong that soon my time is taken up by meetings, conferences, study groups, and workshops that prevent me from walking the streets. It is difficult not to have plans, not to organize people around an urgent cause, and not to feel that you are working directly for social progress. But I wonder more and more if the first thing shouldn't be to know people by name, to eat and drink with them, to listen to their stories and tell your own, and to let them know with words, handshakes, and hugs that you do not simply like them, but truly love them.

In asking God to hear our prayer, we are the agents of God's presence when we visit the lonely, offer strength to all who suffer in mind, body, and spirit and comfort those who are failing and infirm—not as we send God, but as God sends us.

Leonard Hamlin Sr.

Lord Jesus, in Gethsemane, your friends were not able to stay awake and watch with you, and, when you were taken, they all fled leaving you alone; remember with compassion and for good those who are alone; those who have lost friends or family to death; those whose lives have been solitary because of work or particular burdens. We pray also for those who in selfishness or other faults have broken every tie, those whose guilt or sin leaves them alone or despised. We pray for those who have been falsely accused and shunned for no reasons, those embittered through what they have endured, and for all caught in the isolation of mental confusion. In all of these, O Lord, let your Spirit work forgiveness and reconciliation, renewal and hope; give to each of us such a sense of your abiding love, such a confidence in the communion of saints and such a heart that as we turn toward you, we turn also toward each other, in perfect charity and in the bonds of friendship; for you have called us friends and welcome us all into the one and eternal kingdom. Amen.

— Adapted, The People's Missal, 1919

Thursday _____

That it may please thee to support, help,
and comfort all who are in danger, necessity,
and tribulation,

We beseech thee to hear us, good Lord.

So many pundits, opinion writers, and talking heads continue
to remind us of the rising levels of loneliness in our society. In
the most connected world, more people feel alone than ever
before. This fact became even increasingly apparent during the
shutdowns and lockdowns of the COVID-19 pandemic. We
saw time and again how so many people spent days and weeks
without contact with another. And what a travesty that was.

We all need community and support. Studies, doctors, and plain
common sense tell us so. That's not to say we don't also need
time alone for thinking, working, and introspection—we do!
Community matters, though, and especially faith communities.
There is such comfort knowing someone will call on you if
you're sick or send a note after a bad experience or pray with
you. Our faith and belief take us to church, but if there wasn't
something important and necessary about community, we
wouldn't keep coming back.

Our words and prayers today remind us of the importance of this kind of community thinking. There is something quite comforting and universal here. The prayer is not self-involved. In fact, it is for those who may not even know we are praying for them. Our spiritual journey is rooted in seeking support, help, and comfort for others.

There is something fulfilling in this belief of a connection and community that is larger than we can imagine. It helps us see outside of those moments of loneliness and isolation. As we lift up a prayer for someone in danger, necessity, or tribulation, we draw lines of connections.

The world really is a small place. Its expansiveness may seem foreign and daunting, but when we remember to pray for each other, the connections begin to form.

MARGARET RAWLS

O God, you have made of one blood all the peoples of the earth, and sent your blessed Son to preach peace to those who are far off and to those who are near: Grant that people everywhere may seek after you and find you, bring the nations into your fold, pour out your Spirit upon all flesh, and hasten the coming of your kingdom; through Jesus Christ our Lord, who lives and reigns with you and the Holy Spirit, one God, now and for ever. Amen.

—The Book of Common Prayer, p. 257

Hear Us, Good Lord

Friday

That it may please thee to have mercy
upon all mankind,

We beseech thee to hear us, good Lord.

Oh, good Lord, have mercy on us all. There is hardly anything
to add, living as we do under threat of increasing natural
disasters, the disappearance of species, rising sea levels—and
that's just what we've done to the planet. To one another, we
have imposed hierarchies, conditions, wealth and poverty, life
and death according to arbitrary notions of skin color, gender,
and love. What else is there to say, but "Good Lord, have mercy
on us all"?

The Great Litany lays bare our inability to love one another
as God would have us do. This is us, as we are, individually
and collectively. "Have mercy!" is an honest and grief-stricken
response to pain, a recognition that we fall short, again
and again.

This very acknowledgment of pain contains our goodness. If we
did not aspire, however imperfectly, to well-being and delight
and joy and fulfillment for each other, then we would not
cry mercy. We would simply not bother. Seeing the pain and
knowing we could do so much better is what makes us cry,

Mercy, good Lord, have mercy.

Have mercy on us as we love one another and hurt those we love.

Have mercy on us as we desire to do better and conspire with death.

Have mercy on us as we hold both the beauty and the pain of this world.

Have mercy on us as we grieve what we've lost and yearn for new life.

Have mercy on us as we pray and dance and write and imagine and work, and sing and love our way forward, becoming to one another as you are to us.

We beseech thee to hear us, good Lord.

MICHELLE DIBBLEE

Lord, make us instruments of your peace. Where there is hatred, let us sow love; where there is injury, pardon; where there is discord, union; where there is doubt, faith; where there is despair, hope; where there is sadness, joy. Grant that we may not so much seek to be consoled as to console; to be understood as to understand; to be loved as to love. For it is in giving that we receive; it is in pardoning that we are pardoned; and it is in dying that we are born to eternal life. Amen.

—Prayer attributed to Saint Francis,
The Book of Common Prayer, p. 833 (adapted)

Saturday

That it may please thee to give us true repentance;
to forgive us all our sins, negligences, and ignorances;
and to endue us with the grace of thy Holy Spirit
to amend our lives according to thy holy Word,

We beseech thee to hear us, good Lord.

I'm probably not alone in being uncomfortable talking about sin. Our culture so often associates sin with personal moral transgressions that the very word has become sticky with shame.

However, the Greek word the gospel writers most often use for sin means "to miss the mark." Rather than a dualistic interpretation of right or wrong, this definition of sin considers all the ways in which we don't live into our authentic selves, created in the image of God. It offers us the spaciousness to allow for our imperfection as well as our ignorance, to acknowledge the things we have done and left undone, and the grace to do better.

It wasn't until I started a regular practice of contemplative prayer that I started viewing sin through this wider lens, one that helped me develop a more nuanced understanding of the word. One such practice is *lectio divina*. Each Tuesday evening for more than a decade, I have gathered with a community from the cathedral, in-person before the pandemic and later online, to listen for how the Holy Spirit is speaking to us through scripture.

During this time of holy reading, we move through a process of deep listening, using the gospel lesson for the coming Sunday. We reflect on and share the wisdom a particular word or phrase is holding for us—the connections and associations, the way this gem of scripture is shining light on a situation in our lives. We listen for the invitation the Holy Spirit is offering us through our word, be it a prayer, something to ponder further, or, quite often, a call to amend our lives through action or change. And we hold each other in silence, honoring our intentions to be open to the movement of the Spirit in our lives before ending by saying together the prayer that Jesus taught his disciples in which we ask for forgiveness for ourselves and offer forgiveness for others. Like other contemplative practices, *lectio divina* transforms the sharp edges of our brokenness into openings for God's love and forgiveness to enter, and in doing so, calls us to see the world as God sees it.

TERRI LYNN SIMPSON

Our Father, who art in heaven, hallowed be thy Name, thy kingdom come, thy will be done, on earth as it is in heaven. Give us this day our daily bread. And forgive us our trespasses, as we forgive those who trespass against us. And lead us not into temptation, but deliver us from evil. For thine is the kingdom, and the power, and the glory, for ever and ever. Amen.

The Fifth Week of Lent

Sunday

That it may please thee to forgive our enemies, persecutors, and slanderers, and to turn their hearts,

We beseech thee to hear us, good Lord.

From an early age, we begin to understand concepts like kindness, helping, cooperation, and sharing. We learn about the world around us through play and plenty of trial and error. At two- or three-years old, we find a bit of relief in our new understanding that everyone makes mistakes.

It takes a bit longer for us to understand the social value of forgiveness. Innately self-focused as toddlers, most children feel persecuted when wronged and are not yet fully able to consider the feelings of all parties in a conflict or understand the idea of being sorry for what one has done. However, a 2019 psychology study showed that four- and five-year-old children begin to understand forgiveness. The five-year-old children in the study consistently responded positively to a character who forgives.

Learning to forgive friends and classmates for minor transgressions is part of growing up. The adults in our lives, if we are lucky, do their best to teach us right from wrong. As we grow up, we learn about morality and goodness. We learn about moral failings and evil.

But forgiving enemies, persecutors, and slanderers? Even as we grow into adulthood, this is more difficult for us. We dwell on our hurt feelings. We aren't sure why we should forgive.

Yet, if we do forgive, we are pleasantly surprised by our relief from rumination and resentment. This is one of the reasons why we should forgive: it is freeing, for us, and for the person being forgiven. We may even feel momentarily virtuous at having been able to bring ourselves to fully forgive, and this is ok. We can allow ourselves that little pat on the back. Forgiveness is not always easy, but it is a gift, not only to the person we are forgiving but also to ourselves.

The Gospel of Matthew reminds us not only to forgive our enemies but also to love them, saying that God makes the "sun rise on the evil and on the good, and sends rain on the righteous and on the unrighteous" (5:45).

As we ask God to forgive, so, too, must we forgive. During this time of repentance, we reflect on our human foibles and those of others. Be of open heart. Harness the freeing power of forgiveness and empower yourself to be fully ready for reconciliation and the joy of Easter.

KATHERINE M. PRENDERGAST

O God, the Father of all, whose Son commanded us to love our enemies: Lead them and us from prejudice to truth; deliver them and us from hatred, cruelty, and revenge; and in your good time enable us all to stand reconciled before you; through Jesus Christ our Lord. Amen.

—The Book of Common Prayer, p. 816

Hear Us, Good Lord

Monday _____

That it may please thee to strengthen such as do stand; to comfort and help the weak-hearted; to raise up those who fall; and finally to beat down Satan under our feet,

We beseech thee to hear us, good Lord.

Litanies find their roots in Jewish culture and worship. Litanies were written in the early church and prayed, often in a solemn procession. The recitation of "asks" to God is made even more relevant and fervent in times of great need. In 590 CE, as a pandemic raged in Rome as the result of an overflowing Tiber River, Pope Gregory the Great ordered the creation and use of a litany begging God's benevolent intervention to save the people.

And so, at the heart of any litany—and of the Anglican Great Litany crafted by Thomas Cranmer—is a series of petitions to God, asking for God's saving action toward distressing situations in the world. There is an almost panicked, desperate urgency in the language of the Great Litany, as if the petitioners are in dire straits and in need of timely intervention by the divine.

Today's particular petition, then, finds its place in what I would call the "beseeching" section of the Litany. "Beseech" is not a verb commonly used in today's world. It brings gravitas to the "ask" being articulated. It is a reminder to God (as if God needs a reminder!), by the one who prays it, that "the people of God" are in need.

This petition to God is also a reminder to us, the pray-ers of the litany, that there are different needs at different times in our lives. Sometimes we find ourselves with a strong place to stand, from which we can reach out to do the work of justice (beating down Satan) and loving the world in God's Name. For those times, we ask for strength (because we need it!) to do that work and that loving with resolve, conviction, and courage.

There are also times when we find ourselves in real need, when we are feeling "weak-hearted" and needing comfort. The "ask" in this particular petition of the litany is, of course, for God to do the comforting of the weak-hearted. But in my reading of it, there is also the implication that part of what God does in "strengthen[ing] such as do stand," is to strengthen the strong so that they too might be empowered to comfort the weak and weak-hearted.

The role of a priest, I learned in seminary, was "to comfort the afflicted, and to afflict the comfortable." When we are strong ourselves, we are called to comfort others; when we are weak, we accept the comfort given by God and by our brothers and sisters in Christ.

Whom do you know to be in need today—and what might you do to comfort them? And if you yourself are in need today, where will you look and listen for comfort being offered to you?

GENE ROBINSON

Hear Us, Good Lord

O God, lover of the strong and the weak, call me to kindness when I am standing tall and strengthen me for service to those who need comfort. When I have fallen and am weak-hearted myself, give me the comfort of your presence, and open my heart to receive comfort from others. Amen.

Tuesday

That it may please thee to grant
to all the faithful departed
eternal life and peace,

We beseech thee to hear us, good Lord.

The question of whether it was suitable to pray for the dead was a source of bitter controversy during the Reformation of the sixteenth century. Much of what the reformers saw as the excesses and distortions of the late Medieval Western church revolved around prayer for the departed and the various practices associated with it. When the first Book of Common Prayer was promulgated in England in 1549, prayers for the dead in the burial liturgy were drastically reduced from the elaborate intercession for the departed characteristic of the Medieval period. In the burial liturgy of the more reformed prayer book of 1552, which would remain the standard burial liturgy for much of the Anglican world for centuries to come, there was no direct prayer at all for the dead. No longer done for the benefit of the deceased, the burial rite was now intended to do something for the living gathered for the occasion, namely, to inspire them to live a more godly life in their remaining time on earth. There was nothing the living could do for the dead. Death was a moment of great separation.

As time passed and the theological concerns of the sixteenth century became increasingly the stuff of history, a revived desire to pray for the dead emerged, mostly from a pastoral, not theological, concern. In Europe, in particular, the devastating death toll of the First World War created an instinctive desire to pray for departed partners, siblings, children, and friends. In the face of such overwhelming loss, there was a deeply felt need to pray, which, I think, points to the fact that many of us feel at various times a mysterious connection between the living and the dead, even if we might not be able to fully explain it.

The catechism of the 1979 Book of Common Prayer of the Episcopal Church includes the question, "Why do we pray for the dead?" and answers it this way: "We pray for them, because we still hold them in our love, and because we trust that in God's presence those who have chosen to serve him will grow in his love, until they see him as he is" (p. 862). To pray for the dead and commend their souls to almighty God is an act of love, placing before God those whom we see no longer but hold close in our hearts. It is an act of faith, as well, as we trust that they are growing ever into the fullness of the God who created, redeemed, and sanctifies them and who welcomes them home into that place of eternal rest and peace, the very paradise of God.

PATRICK KEYSER

Rest eternal grant to them, O Lord; and let light perpetual shine upon them. May the souls of all the departed, through the mercy of God, rest in peace. Amen.

—The Book of Common Prayer, p. 502

Wednesday

That it may please thee to grant that,
in the fellowship of all the saints,
we may attain to thy heavenly kingdom,

We beseech thee to hear us, good Lord.

As I recite the prayer, I take a moment and try to remember all the moments I have said the words. I think about the spaces I have stood inside to say the prayer. My previous place of worship is very different from Washington National Cathedral. It would only take me two minutes to walk from the front of my apartment building, past the bodega, jaywalk across the street, and enter the front door of a small church in a multicultural neighborhood in Queens, New York. Sometimes, despite my proximity, I would be late and sit on a folding chair at the back of the church—or tiptoe to the front. Depending on which service I attended, I would say the prayers in Spanish or English.

Over time, the space and people have changed. So too has the way I navigate my daily life. I have gained experiences I never thought or dreamed of having. I have been molded by my interactions with individuals; my beliefs have shifted from one side to another, and I am constantly changing. And because of this, I am a much different person today than when I was jaywalking to my church in Queens.

Reflecting on who we were in the past and who we are today allows us to acknowledge that we are not the same person we were as a child, or in high school, or as a young adult. We may not walk through the same spaces or interact with the same individuals. We may have moved on or individuals may have passed on. Throughout the constantly shifting, molding, and changing, there is an end to our experiences. Yes, we have grown and changed, but through it all, is the one constant: God.

Whether we attend Washington National Cathedral or a small church just past the bodega, whether we worship with people we have known for years or we are the new face in the crowd, when we worship God, we come together to create community and share a prayer. In these moments as a community, surrounded by those individuals, we are accepted for who we were, are, and will be. There has always been and will be acceptance as we all walk together to the kingdom of God.

JOSEPH PERALTA

Almighty God, the fountain of all wisdom: Enlighten by thy Holy Spirit those who teach and those who learn, that, rejoicing in the knowledge of thy truth, they may worship thee and serve thee from generation to generation; through Jesus Christ our Lord, who liveth and reigneth with thee and the same Spirit, one God, for ever and ever. Amen.

—The Book of Common Prayers, p. 209

Thursday

Son of God, we beseech thee to hear us.

Son of God, we beseech thee to hear us.

The first time I heard words like these in a song, Jesus was wearing a Superman T-shirt, banging on an upright piano.

I am thinking of the iconic Stephen Schwartz musical, *Godspell*, an allegorical, vaudeville-style reenactment of the Gospel of Matthew. The film version begins with people being drawn mysteriously to New York's Central Park fountain, reemerging with new identities.

The song "We Beseech Thee" is an exuberant ensemble number with a show-stopping dance sequence. It occurs long after Jesus experiences his own baptism and dons his Superman shirt, after all the characters enact the parables and begin to understand them, after the foreshadowing when a woman avoids a stoning.

The song is based on a nineteenth-century hymn by Thomas Benson Pollock, which reads like a litany. In the film, singers do a raucous call and response, petitioning for every freedom and forgiveness, each verse ending with a shout. As they dance around the city toward Lincoln Center, you hardly notice the light dimming in the background, preparation for Superman's encounter with a willow tree.

Listening again after many years, I find that I pay less attention to the verses of the song and more to the subtle chorus that builds. Between the shouts, a chorus quietly calls, but the characters are busy running around in their wigs and their costumes, asking for things. They are so busy beseeching that they do not realize that someone or something has been beseeching them, asking them to sing about love.

One of the blessings of time, I guess, is the desire to listen a little more and in all things to try to discern the chorus from the verse. To be sure, it is not every day that I take time to listen, as I have a few things that I have been beseeching for, myself. And even when I do listen, I admit that I do not always hear a love chorus swelling. But every once in a while, it does get through to me.

ELIZABETH JOHNS

Love, that caused us first to be, love, that bled upon the tree, love, that draws us lovingly:

We beseech thee, hear us.

—The Rev. Thomas Benson Pollock

Friday

O Lamb of God, that takest away
the sins of the world,

Have mercy on us.

I have an older brother whom I love and care about but adored even more as a child. He is five years older than my twin sister and me, so I can tell you that while he may also love us, his idea of fun when we were all growing up was certainly not playing with his little sisters. Because there were two of us, it seemed like my brother always had some other pesky friend with whom to play and get into trouble. To my Barbie doll-playing and coloring mind, these activities were foreign.

One such game, which, looking back, is fairly bizarre in that way children's games can be, was called "Mercy." In the game, you and a friend (or opponent) would lock hands and attempt to bend each other's fingers in such a way as to make the other cry mercy. The purpose of the game is obvious, but even to a six-year-old, it seemed, well, dumb. Fear not, the cannonballs at the pool in the summer restored my brother's place as one to be idolized.

We bend ourselves into situations and places that beg us to cry for mercy. We make poor decisions—get in the car when we shouldn't, take a job that isn't fulfilling, continue a relationship that doesn't help us grow. So often, like the game we played as children, it's a matter of pride that keeps us from crying out for mercy. We don't reach out and seek forgiveness or compassion. But that is exactly what we need to do. Life is not a competition, and there are no prizes or bragging rights for holding out.

As we spend the next three days with these words in the Great Litany, I invite you to think about how you can shed your ego and ask for mercy, forgiveness, compassion. Mercy is not to be taken lightly, but it is given to us and for us. These days of Lent can be long as we await the joyous news of Easter, but they teach and prepare us. Let us continue to take this time to learn and practice.

MARGARET RAWLS

Direct us, O Lord, in all our doings with thy most gracious favor, and further us with thy continual help; that in all our works begun, continued, and ended in thee, we may glorify thy holy Name, and finally, by thy mercy, obtain everlasting life; through Jesus Christ our Lord. Amen.

—The Book of Common Prayer, p. 832

Saturday

O Lamb of God, that takest away
the sins of the world,

Have mercy upon us.

We have John the Baptist to thank for this language of Jesus as the "Lamb of God who takes away the sin of the world" (John 1:29). Referring to Jesus as a lamb is intentional. The Old Testament has several passages that provide context to the cultural understanding of the sacrificial lamb at the time that the Gospel according to John was written. Exodus 29:38 provides instruction for sacrificing lambs daily, and Isaiah 53:7 refers to a figure who was led like a lamb to slaughter.

Jesus was a Jewish man living in a culture that recognized the innocence of a lamb and the significance of sacrificing lambs in worship to the God of the Israelites. These passages can help illuminate the context of the words of John the Baptist, but they should not be read with a supersessionist lens that appropriates Jewish text for Christian purposes.

In our modern context, the imagery of the lamb is somewhat less salient because animal sacrifice is far less common. However, I invite you to take some time today, during this season of Lent, to reflect on what it means to call the Son of God the "Lamb of

God." What does it mean to equate God's own incarnate form with something like a sacrificial lamb? Such an implication gives meaning to the claim in our litany that Jesus is the one "who takest away the sins of the world." His sacrifice meant something and continues to mean something.

I have heard some describe "sin" as a "turning away from God." Jesus's sacrifice gives us an opportunity to turn back to God. As we move through these final days of Lent and pray through the Great Litany, consider what Jesus's sacrifice means to you in your life. I invite you to take some time to pray with Jesus and this imagery of the sacrificial lamb. Try exploring John 1:29 (and the surrounding verses) through the practice of *Lectio Divina*, Ignatian Imagination, or another way of engaging the scripture. Then, ask Jesus to have mercy upon you. Maybe you have a specific reason in mind or simply offer the words as a general petition, but I encourage you to allow yourself to be moved by such a prayer. How do you feel?

JACQUELINE GALVINHILL

Almighty God, who hast promised to hear the petitions of those who ask in thy Son's Name: We beseech thee mercifully to incline thine ear to us who have now made our prayers and supplications unto thee; and grant that those things which we have faithfully asked according to thy will, may effectually be obtained, to the relief of our necessity, and to the setting forth of thy glory; through Jesus Christ our Lord. Amen.

—The Book of Common Prayer, p. 834

Palm Sunday_____

O Lamb of God, that takest away
the sins of the world,

Grant us thy peace.

Upon seeing Jesus, John the Baptist exclaims, "Here is the Lamb
of God who takes away the sin of the world!" (John 1:29).
John proclaims the central truth of our faith: Jesus's death as
the Lamb of God is the ultimate demonstration of God's love.
We who have been held captive by sin and death have been
emancipated, "not with perishable things like silver or gold, but
with the precious blood of Christ, like that of a lamb without
defect or blemish" (1 Peter 1:18-19). The Lamb's power comes
through slaughter. He conquers through death, not of others,
but of his own. "I [John] saw between the throne and the four
living creatures and among the elders a Lamb standing as if
it had been slaughtered," whose blood "ransomed for God
saints from every tribe and language and people and nation"
(Revelation 5:6, 9). The Lamb of God dies and rises for our
salvation, bringing us joys of eternal life, granting us peace.

On Palm Sunday, the Lamb's path to slaughter starts off in
earnest. The imagery is confusing, dizzying, and disturbing.

We begin in riotous joy, as we teeter on the edge of shame and death. We welcome Jesus as a king, yet our king arrives on a borrowed donkey. The mood is jubilant, yet all is draped in red symbolizing the blood of the martyrs. Ringing songs of praise are metamorphosed into screams calling for death. Before this week is finished, the Lamb will be tried, condemned, dispossessed, tortured, and crucified until death.

We are called to take our part in the cosmic drama unfolding before us, a drama set before the foundations of the world. We must journey with Jesus on these difficult days ahead. We must resist the impulse to turn away, only to reemerge on Easter Day with its orderly, sanitized magnificence. We are invited to share a meal with Jesus like the disciples. Like his mother and the other women, we must keep vigil at the foot of the cross. Like Joseph, we are called to prepare and bury his body.

Following the ignominious death of Jesus, the hopes of many of his followers were crushed. This is a familiar feeling today. In a world where we are constantly and forcibly reminded of our frailty, our mortality, and the injustices in the ordering of our common life, hope can be in scarce supply. Only after entering the stunning sweep of Holy Week, can we, like the stunned myrrh-bearers and apostles, proclaim the resurrection in next Sunday's dark early hours.

TORRENCE N. THOMAS

Almighty and everliving God, in your tender love for the human race you sent your Son our Savior Jesus Christ to take upon him our nature, and to suffer death upon the cross, giving us the example of his great humility: Mercifully grant that we may walk in the way of his suffering, and also share in his resurrection; through Jesus Christ our Lord, who lives and reigns with you and the Holy Spirit, one God, for ever and ever. Amen.

—The Book of Common Prayer, p. 219

Monday of Holy Week _____

O Christ, hear us.

O Christ, hear us.

In the Great Litany, we have prayed for deliverance from our sins and have beseeched God to hear us as we prayed for God's blessings for ourselves and others. We have asked the Lamb of God for mercy and peace. Now we ask Christ to hear us. This seems like such a simple request, but it is more than that.

We want to be heard. We desire for others not just to listen to our words but to really hear and truly understand what we are saying, what we mean. We want those with whom we speak in more than casual conversation to "get us," to read between the lines and know the depth and truth of what we are saying even if, perhaps especially if, we can't articulate it ourselves.

We need not be cogent when we pray. Prayers that are a rambling mess are perfectly acceptable. In Jesus's parable of a Pharisee and a tax collector in the temple (Luke 18:9-14), the latter was justified because his simple prayer, "God, be merciful to me, a sinner," was prayed from his heart, from a place of humbling himself before God.

We sinful humans carry the weight of our sin within us. It is difficult to look at, even harder to speak aloud. Perhaps we are afraid to say the words and thus own the sin. Perhaps we don't know how to forgive those who have sinned against us. Perhaps we need help from God but don't know how to ask for it or don't know what to ask for or don't feel that we deserve it. Perhaps we don't want to look at our participation in, or benefit from, institutional sins like racism that are difficult to face honestly. Saint Paul reminds us that "the Spirit helps us in our weakness; for we do not know how to pray as we ought, but that very Spirit intercedes with sighs too deep for words" (Romans 8:26). We don't need words to pray if we don't have them.

We can have great hope. We believe in a God who knows both our light and our shadows—and loves us infinitely more than we can understand. We can pray, "Christ, hear us," and know that Christ does indeed hear us and understands us and knows our needs. Jesus knows what we are afraid to look at, what hurts us to think about, what we don't know how to pray about, and what we don't even realize we need to pray about.

Let us pray, "O Christ, hear us," with confidence.

Thanks be to God!

Michael Lewallen

*Almighty and everlasting God, you are always more ready to hear
than we to pray, and to give more than we either desire or deserve:
Pour upon us the abundance of your mercy, forgiving us those things
of which our conscience is afraid, and giving us those good things
for which we are not worthy to ask, except through the merits and
mediation of Jesus Christ our Savior; who lives and reigns with you
and the Holy Spirit, one God, for ever and ever.* Amen.

—The Book of Common Prayer, p. 234

Tuesday of Holy Week _____

Lord, have mercy upon us. Kyrie eleison.

Christ, have mercy upon us. Christe eleison.

Lord, have mercy upon us. Kyrie eleison.

We were about a dozen gathered that afternoon, in March, probably. It was warm enough not to feel a draft through the leaded windowpanes and light enough not to need the fluorescents overhead. We sat behind heavy wood tables in a u-shape, all following along as he read aloud. I can't recall his name, but I can tell you that his piece was about the day he received his first bicycle. At fourteen years old.

When the reading concluded and the workshop was to begin, there was a long pause. Another classmate looked around the room a few times, as though preparing to cross a busy street, before offering, "I really enjoyed this. I actually didn't learn how to ride a bike until I was pretty old too. So, the feeling is spot on." The floodgates opened. Five or more late-blooming bikers emerged from anonymity in this most unlikely place, swapping stories of scabbed knees and Sisyphean embarrassment.

Most people don't bike every day or even every week; we should be forgiven for herky-jerky starts and occasionally dismounting to walk up steep hills. And late bloomers especially should be forgiven for our reluctance to describe things of perceived universal ease as "just like riding a bike." It takes us time to overcome shame and the need to ask for help. We need time to admit to our failure and find comfort in the discovery that we are not alone.

Most people don't hear or speak Greek or Latin every day, or week, or month, or perhaps more than the two or three times a year they come to church on special occasions. Yet, these words—*Kyrie eleison, Christe eleison, Kyrie eleison*—swell almost immediately in our hearts and on our lips. Each invitation and response gets louder, stronger, and more familiar. The affirmation, conviction, and necessity build like those first, smooth, powerful pedal strokes after the chain clicks into the right gear.

In theory, praying these words is something we all know how to do but don't do (or at least not often enough). The mechanics are simple; the tools are basic. We're told that it's easy though not effortless, which we believe sometimes and not others. Even for the best among us, getting started is always awkward. And, if we stop, for no matter how long, when we begin again, we will all do it in exactly the same way.

In theory, asking for mercy is just like riding a bike.

GABRIELLE McKENZIE

May the Lord support us all the day long, till the shades lengthen and the evening comes, and the busy world is hushed, and the fever of life is over, and our work is done. Then in his mercy may he give us a safe lodging, and holy rest, and peace at the last. Amen.

—Cardinal John Henry Newman

Wednesday of Holy Week_____

*Our Father, who art in heaven, hallowed be thy Name,
thy kingdom come, thy will be done, on earth as it is in
heaven. Give us this day our daily bread. And forgive
us our trespasses, as we forgive those who trespass against
us. And lead us not into temptation, but deliver us from
evil.* Amen.

I have built many pieces of Ikea furniture in my days, and it
always goes the same: I open all the packaging and lay out the
materials. Then I take a glance at the cover of the instruction
manual and put it in the recycle bin. Away I go with my
screwdriver and Allen wrench, and about halfway through, I
become frustrated because it doesn't look right, or some screws
don't fit the holes. Exasperated, I admit defeat. Eventually I dig
out the manual from the bin and start over properly, and all's
well that ends well! Now, if Jesus were sitting there watching
me, I imagine he would point me to Matthew 6:7-15. To me,
this passage of scripture boils down to Jesus telling us: *use the
manual I have given you. Don't just attempt to pray (or build
furniture); use the instructions given within.*

In the Gospel of Matthew, Jesus says to his disciples, "Do not
heap up empty phrases as the Gentiles do; for they think that
they will be heard because of their many words. Do not be like
them, for your Father knows what you need before you ask him"

(Matthew 6:7-8). In the next verse, he instructs the disciples: "Pray then in this way." This is our instruction manual. This is our guide to prayer.

We dedicate and direct the prayer to "Our Father, who art in heaven." We give reverence to God: "hallowed be thy Name." With the words, "thy kingdom come, thy will be done, on earth as it is in heaven," we ask God for guidance in our daily lives so we can be part of the holy city. God's will reigns in heaven with justice and compassion, and we pray that we may do so here on earth as well. Next, we ask God for nourishment of the soul, and then we ask for the forgiveness of others, while, harder yet, we try to forgive those who have harmed us. We ask God to lead us away from sin, and from there, we move into asking God to forgive us for our transgressions, praying that they do not lead us into a lifetime of falling into sin. Finally, we close our prayer with "Amen," which means "so be it." With this word, we ratify our prayer.

This Lent, instead of just reciting these words, I invite you to take a moment to think about each petition and its meaning. Think about what you are praying for in each phrase and ask yourself if you are following Jesus's instruction manual in your daily life.

MEGAN A. BLELLOCH

*Almighty and everlasting God, by whose Spirit the whole body
of your faithful people is governed and sanctified: Receive our
supplications and prayers, which we offer before you for all members
of your holy Church, that in their vocation and ministry they may
truly and devoutly serve you; through our Lord and Savior Jesus
Christ, who lives and reigns with you, in the unity of the Holy
Spirit, one God, now and for ever.* Amen.

—The Book of Common Prayer, p. 256-57

Maundy Thursday_____

O Lord, let thy mercy be showed upon us;

As we do put our trust in thee.

It seems fitting and proper that as our Lenten pilgrimage draws to a close, this last petition of the Great Litany, with its plea for God's mercy and our trust, be set for Maundy Thursday. If there is ever a time that we need to trust in God's love, grace, and mercy, it is this day when our Lord instituted the sacrament of his body and blood that brings with it our new life in Christ.

Jesus gathers his closest friends around him. He calls them together to strengthen and prepare them for the days to come, but he also gathers them together to say goodbye.

Jesus tells them, "You are those who have stood by me in my trials; and I confer on you, just as my Father has conferred on me, a kingdom" (Luke 22:28-29).

We are left only with a fragment of the words and actions of our Lord during these final days. But a fragment is enough, and in his words and actions, we see his care of and concern, not only for his disciples but also for each one of us who trust in his love, grace, and mercy.

"You call me Teacher and Lord—and you are right, for that is what I am. So if I, your Lord and Teacher, have washed your feet, you also ought to wash one another's feet. For I have set you an example, that you also should do as I have done to you" (John 13:13-15).

There is simplicity, an obvious theme, to his words and actions that, in retrospect, is easy for us to understand. We can never really know what the word and actions of Jesus at that evening meal meant to the disciples. But he left us with a clear picture of how we are to live our lives: "The greatest among you must become like the youngest, and the leader like one who serves" (Luke 22:26).

Our Lord calls us to a servanthood that is inclusive and open to all we meet along life's path. He sets before us a clear example of how we should live with and among others.

We are the grateful recipients of the ancient ceremony that the disciples of Jesus participated in on that fateful night. For us, as it became for them, the eucharistic meal is the living reminder that our Lord is ever present among us, and the foot washing of Maundy Thursday is a yearly call to the servanthood of all believers.

May God grant us the wisdom and grace to approach every eucharist with a renewed sense of our Lord's presence among us. Trusting in God's gracious mercy, may we actively live our servanthood all the days of our life.

PRESTON B. HANNIBAL

Holy God, your knowledge of me exceeds what I grasp or see in any moment; you know me better than I know myself. Now, help me to trust in your mercy, to see myself in the light of your holiness, and grant me the grace that I may have true contrition, make an honest confession, and find in you forgiveness and perfect remission. Amen.

—*Saint Augustine's Prayer Book*, p. 120

Good Friday

Let us pray.

Time and time again I have heard these words spoken. I have read these words from the printed pages of programs, novels, and most pointedly sacred texts. These are words that have been offered to me as an individual and as part of an assembly gathered in hope of being connected as community. "Let us pray" are words that have been shared in small groups, across dinner tables filled with familiar faces, family members, and strangers who would become friends. Reading or hearing these words in this moment surfaces a multitude of occasions that fill my head and my heart.

In my life, these words have been most impactful when they were offered as an invitation. We are presented with an opportunity to step into a transformational moment when we humble ourselves in prayer. The past, present, and future miraculously intermingle as the mental and emotional walls we built are removed. We begin to imagine and believe in powerful possibilities as our faith is stirred through divine conversation with God. Even in the bleakest of moments, I have heard these words reminding me there is always a bright side somewhere.

Our lives are filled with appointments, responsibilities, and obligations. So many of these are of our own making and become obstacles to hearing the invitation clearly and grasping the opportunity to be spiritually strengthened. We should respond to these words not because we hear them as an obligation but more importantly as an invitation. As Bill Hybels, author of *Too Busy Not To Pray*, cautions, "God doesn't want us to pile up impressive phrases. He doesn't want us to use words without thinking about their meaning. He wants us to talk to him as to a friend or father—authentically, reverently, personally, earnestly."

On this Good Friday, let us hear the invitation to draw closer in conversation and relationship with God, knowing that there is power in prayer. Let us pray that we might be imbued with the power to transform our circumstances, to find what unites rather than divides us, and to be moved to help the poor, the needy, the marginalized, ostracized, dishonored, and disinherited.

We are invited on this day to pray not that we might see prayer as an instrument to change others or the circumstances around us but rather as an opportunity to be in the presence of the one whose divine power transforms us.

LEONARD L. HAMLIN SR.

Lord Jesus Christ, you bore our condemnation on the cross; give me a heart that is broken for the wrong I have done, the harm I have caused others, the good I have not done, and, most of all, that I have turned away from you. For these, and for any sins I cannot now remember, and for any failure to recognize and acknowledge my sins, I truly and humbly repent and ask mercy. Give me sorrow for all my sins and trust in your forgiveness. Amen.

—Saint Augustine's Prayer Book, p. 132

Holy Saturday _____

*Almighty God, who hast promised to hear the petitions
of those who ask in thy Son's Name: We beseech thee
mercifully to incline thine ear to us who have now
made our prayers and supplications unto thee; and
grant that those things which we have asked faithfully
according to thy will, may be obtained effectually, to
the relief of our necessity, and to the setting forth of thy
glory; through Jesus Christ our Lord.* Amen.

This concluding collect of the Great Litany appropriately comes
at the end of the prayer petitions and on Holy Saturday, the day
before the resurrection of our Lord. It also comes at the end of
our Lenten journey, a season when we have reflected upon the
various twists and turns of our lives as we journey with Jesus to
Calvary and the cross. In this prayer, we "beseech" God to hear
us and pray that God will "grant that those things which we
have asked faithfully…may be obtained effectually."

Beseeching God to hear us reminds me of one of the best-
known and beloved refrains from the Taizé tradition, "O Lord,
Hear My Prayer."

*O Lord, hear my prayer, O Lord, hear my prayer;
When I call answer me. O Lord, hear my prayer,
O Lord, hear my prayer; Come and listen to me.*

On this last day of Lent, we seek to gather up in prayer all that we have experienced, asking God for forgiveness and a new life in Christ. We find ourselves in that in-between time—between the cross and the resurrection. A Forward Movement writer put it this way, "The truth is, we often live in between times, when the old has died but the new has yet to come…There is a gap between where we are—physically, emotionally, spiritually—and where we want to be. Could it be that this is exactly where God wants us? Today is a day for letting go, for accepting our lives as they are—however incomplete and transitory they seem to be—and waiting for the new life that is to come."

As we close out this Lenten journey, we remember that God hears our prayers and that God loved us enough to take on flesh and dwell among us so our lives would never be the same. As the theologian Henri Nouwen said, "The miracle of the incarnation is not only that Christ came, lived, died and rose among us, but Christ continues to come, to live, to die, and to rise in our midst." Thanks be to God!

JAN NAYLOR COPE

O God, Creator of heaven and earth: Grant that, as the crucified body of your dear Son was laid in the tomb and rested on this holy Sabbath, so we may await with him the coming of the third day, and rise with him to newness of life; who now lives and reigns with you and the Holy Spirit, one God, for ever and ever. Amen.

—The Book of Common Prayer, p. 283

Easter
Day

Easter Day

The grace of our Lord Jesus Christ, and the love of God, and the fellowship of the Holy Ghost, be with us all evermore. *Amen.*

The forty days are over. The Lenten journey has come to an end. Easter is here and with it our celebration of the most unexpected, unfathomable, undeserved, and extraordinary event in human history. Christ is risen! As twentieth-century theologian Frederick Buechner once said, "If it is true, there is nothing left to say. If it is not true, there is nothing left to say."

Easter is the Christian version of the mic drop. Easter is God's refusal to let evil win; more importantly, it is God's refusal to let love lose. Jesus came among us to show us what it means to be truly human. He came to show us the way of love. But we took him and nailed him to a tree, unable to stomach the truth he showed us about ourselves. And that is where it should have ended. Jesus should have been just another good man brought down by a world that prefers power over peace, a world that stones the prophets and kills God's messengers, as Jesus himself reminded us.

But the thing is, our God is always working to redeem the broken, the lost, the unjust. Our God is always working to reconcile the sin that separates and destroys. As a result, on Easter, God took the crucifixion and stood it on its head. God transformed it from the most heinous form of execution into the means by which the whole world is saved. We killed Jesus, but rather than punish us for that atrocity, God raised Jesus from the grave, and in so doing, destroyed death. We killed Jesus, but rather than put us to death for such a betrayal, God promises us that we too will rise from the grave never to taste death again.

The empty tomb, the risen Christ, the proclamation that life is stronger than death, that love wins in the end…Easter is a crazy story, but it is one that has saved my life and it just might save yours. It is up to you to decide what you will make of this day. Easter can be just a celebration of spring, a beloved holiday to gather family and friends together, a chance to sing some favorite hymns and see the church decked out in flowers. That's the easy way out. But what if by some crazy unimaginable act of love, Easter is all true? Then we have every reason to hope, every reason to laugh, every reason to lift our faces to heaven and shout with countless others over the centuries: *Alleluia. Christ is risen. The Lord is risen indeed. Alleluia.*

RANDOLPH MARSHALL HOLLERITH

Almighty God, who through your only-begotten Son Jesus Christ overcame death and opened to us the gate of everlasting life: Grant that we, who celebrate with joy the day of the Lord's resurrection, may be raised from the death of sin by your life-giving Spirit; through Jesus Christ our Lord, who lives and reigns with you and the Holy Spirit, one God, now and for ever. Amen.

—The Book of Common Prayer, p. 222

Hear Us, Good Lord

About the Authors _____

Megan A. Blelloch joined Washington National Cathedral in 2018 as a congregation member and in 2021 became part of the cathedral's development office as a prospect research analyst. A graduate of American University, she received her undergraduate degree in international studies from American's School of International Service. Additionally, she is set to complete her graduate certificate in paralegal studies from Villanova University in December 2022. In her free time, Megan enjoys traveling and exploring new places, reading, and cooking.

Jan Naylor Cope is provost of Washington National Cathedral where she oversees the development department and works closely with the dean and the cathedral's leadership on its strategic vision, ministry, and mission. Prior to ordained ministry, she served on the senior staff in the White House and as president of her executive search firm.

Jan serves as an officer of the Compass Rose Society, an international outreach organization supporting the Archbishop of Canterbury and the Anglican Communion. She is an adjunct professor of preaching at Wesley Theological Seminary and editor of *Reconciliation, Healing, and Hope: Sermons from*

Washington National Cathedral. Jan is a frequent guest preacher and speaker nationally and internationally, and she lives with her husband, John, in Washington, D.C.

Dana Corsello has served as the vicar of Washington National Cathedral since July 2017. She pastors the cathedral congregation of 1,350 local members, and now, with the help of her clergy colleagues, a growing online congregation of national and international viewers.

During the 24 years of her ordained ministry, she has also served parishes in Tuxedo Park, New York, Richmond, Virginia, and San Francisco, California.

Michelle Dibblee joined the cathedral staff in 2016 and leads the cathedral's civic programming, including events related to veterans and racial justice, interfaith, and other faith and public life content. Before coming to the cathedral, Michelle spent more than 15 years in nonprofit work and community organizing in Minnesota and New York City. She lives in Washington, D.C., with her wife, the Rev. Michele Morgan.

 **Kelly Brown Douglas** serves as the dean of the Episcopal Divinity School at Union Theological Seminary and the Bill and Judith Moyers Chair in Theology at Union. She also is canon theologian at the Washington National Cathedral and theologian in residence at Trinity Church Wall Street. Her academic work has focused on womanist theology, sexuality and the Black church, and racial and social justice. She is the author of many articles and books, including *Resurrection Hope: A Future Where Black Lives Matter, Stand Your Ground: Black Bodies and the Justice of God*, and *Sexuality and the Black Church: A Womanist Perspective*.

In addition to preaching in pulpits across the nation and speaking at universities and other institutions around the globe, Kelly is a frequent and vocal presence in today's print, broadcast, and digital public square, speaking on racial and social justice, among other matters. At the time of her 1983 ordination, she was one of the first ten Black women ordained in the Episcopal Church. She holds a master's degree in theology and a doctorate in systematic theology from Union Theological Seminary.

 **Rosemarie Logan Duncan** joined the staff of Washington National Cathedral as canon for worship in 2016 and is responsible for overseeing all aspects of the cathedral's worship life. A native Washingtonian and cradle Episcopalian, she previously served as associate rector at St. Columba's Episcopal Church in Washington, D.C., for 11 years.

She received her bachelor, master, and doctorate degrees in psychology from Howard University and master of divinity and doctor of ministry degrees from Virginia Theological Seminary. Prior to ordination to the priesthood in 2006, she was a church musician and clinical psychologist. She resides in Washington with her wife.

Jacqueline Galvinhill began serving as the cathedral's seminarian in the Fall of 2021. She graduated from College of the Holy Cross in 2018, having majored in religious studies with a concentration in gender, sexuality, and women's studies. After college, she spent two years serving with the Episcopal Service Corps where her work included serving as the evangelism coordinator for Christ Church Cathedral, Springfield, Massachusetts. She is working on her master of divinity degree at Virginia Theological Seminary and is a postulant for ordination in the Diocese of Western Massachusetts.

Leonard L. Hamlin Sr. was appointed the canon missioner of the Washington National Cathedral in March 2018 and serves as the minister of equity and inclusion. He oversees the Washington National Cathedral's outreach and social justice initiatives, including gun violence prevention and racial justice and reconciliation. Leonard assists in developing relationships and building partnerships for equipping the cathedral community and the congregation to serve in local, regional, and national communities. He received his bachelor, master of divinity, and doctor of ministry degrees from Howard University.

Preston B. Hannibal retired as associate for pastoral care at Washington National Cathedral. Prior to joining the cathedral staff, he served as canon for academic ministries in the Episcopal Diocese of Washington. His ministry has primarily been in secondary schools and college settings. He is co-founder of The Bishop John T. Walker School for Boys and for the past 16 years, chief among his commitments has been the school's growth and development. Its mission is to serve the boys of traditionally underserved Washington, D.C., communities who would not ordinarily have a chance to attend a school of its caliber. Preston lives in Washington with his wife, Sandi.

Yoimel González Hernández serves as the dean of the Latino Deacon's School in the Diocese of Washington. Born in Cuba, he graduated from the Seminario Evangélico de Teología de Matanzas, and from Virginia Theological Seminary. He was ordained to the priesthood in 2019. Along with diocesan responsibilities, he works in youth and Latino ministries at St. Alban's Episcopal Church in Washington, D.C. He has collaborated with the initiative Baptized for Life/Vida en Abundancia as a catechist, and he has represented the wider church as an alternate deputy to General

Convention (Baltimore, 2022) and as a delegate to the World Council of Churches General Assembly (Germany, 2022). He is passionate for social justice, community building, multicultural ministries, and Bible study.

Born and raised in Baton Rouge, Louisiana, **Melissa Hollerith** received her undergraduate degree from Tulane University and a master of divinity degree from Yale University. Ordained an Episcopal priest in 1992, she is also married to a priest, Randy Hollerith. They have two adult children, Marshall and Eliza, and a beloved black Labrador, Lady. Melissa has three decades of ordained ministry under her belt and is currently serving as a chaplain and teacher in the upper school at St. Albans School in Washington, D.C.

Melissa credits her mother who started the first food bank in the state of Louisiana in their family's garage as her best role model for servant ministry. She enjoys good Louisiana cooking and watching SEC football, especially the LSU Tigers.

Randolph "Randy" Marshall Hollerith was named the eleventh dean of Washington National Cathedral in 2016. He holds degrees from Denison University and Yale Divinity School. During his tenure, he has led the creation of a five-year strategic plan, raised $27 million for the renovation of the Cathedral College, overseen budget growth from $14 million to $23 million, and reoriented the institution toward radical welcome and hospitality, with a particular focus on racial reconciliation. Randy is married to the Rev. Melissa Hollerith and is the proud father of two adult children.

Elizabeth Johns serves as development writer and institutional voice of the cathedral. She writes and tracks business proposals, drawing on experience with large, international organizations. In her spare time, she enjoys developing creative people, working on projects across a range of media.

Patrick Keyser joined Washington National Cathedral as priest associate in September 2019. A Virginia native, Patrick graduated from the College of William and Mary. He received his master of divinity degree from Yale Divinity School with a diploma in Anglican studies from Berkeley Divinity School. He was ordained priest in the Diocese of Virginia in 2019.

Lauralyn Lee was named permanent chief of staff and chief operating officer in January 2022, charged with guiding the cathedral staff during a period of intense transition and reorganization as the cathedral weathered the pandemic and opened its doors to the public. Lauralyn is no stranger to the cathedral; she and her husband, Peter Lee, were married at the cathedral, they baptized their children here, and their two daughters attend National Cathedral School. She previously served as a contractor for the dean to help shape the cathedral's 2019–2023 Strategic Plan.

Lauralyn has spent the last several years working as a management consultant to large mission-driven institutions (churches, museums, and universities). A lawyer by training, she worked for nearly two decades at Georgetown University, serving first in the Office of University Counsel and later as a senior administrator with responsibility for community engagement and master planning. The Arizona native attended college at Arizona State University and received a law degree from Duke University.

 **Michael Lewallen** has worked in human resources at the cathedral since 2002. He is a lifelong church musician, having served most recently as the director of music at Advent Lutheran Church in Arlington, Virginia, for 18 years. He has sung with several choral ensembles in the D.C. metro area. Together with his husband, he has performed with The Washington Revels since 2004. He attended Randolph-Macon College and Shenandoah College and Conservatory of Music (now Shenandoah University). He is the proud parent of a son and is a doting granddaddy.

Gabrielle McKenzie leads the donor relations and stewardship program at Washington National Cathedral, bridging the supporter experience from direct mail to major gifts. In this role, she also directs copy and design of major donor publications and frequently writes for leadership. Prior to joining the Washington National Cathedral staff in 2017, she worked in executive support and development for various art museums and performing arts institutions in the Washington, D.C., and Boston areas. She earned a bachelor's degree in English and economics from Boston College and master's degree in finance from Georgetown University.

Joseph Peralta has been the director of the Cathedral Scholars Program for six years. He previously worked in college readiness programs at the Posse Foundation and For Love of Children, building experiences in mentoring students (even after the college selection process), recruiting volunteers and community leaders to engage with the students, and launching an after-school program for college access and financial aid assistance for low-income families. He has spent his career working with students from across the social, economic, and academic spectrum and guiding them through the college process as well as mentoring them throughout their college career.

Katherine M. Prendergast serves as director for the Office of the Dean at Washington National Cathedral. In addition to supporting the dean and provost in their priestly duties, she communicates on their behalf with a variety of constituencies and serves as a liaison to governance and volunteer groups supporting the cathedral.

A graduate of Kent Place School in Summit, New Jersey, Kathy has a bachelor's degree in English language and literature from Smith College and a master's degree in education from The George Washington University. Her interests include music, cooking, gardening, and spending time near the sea.

Margaret Rawls joined the cathedral in 2018 and currently works in the dean's office as the special projects and institutional initiatives manager. A graduate of the University of Virginia, she received her undergraduate degree in religious studies and a master's degree in religion, politics, and conflict focusing her research on Confederate memorials and contested sacred sites.

 **V. Gene Robinson** was elected bishop of the Episcopal Diocese of New Hampshire on June 7, 2003, becoming the first openly gay and partnered bishop in historic Christianity. He retired from that position in early 2013. In 2017, he became vice president of religion and senior pastor at Chautauqua Institution, having served for nearly five years as a senior fellow at the Center for American Progress, Washington, D.C. He authored *In the Eye of the Storm: Swept to the Center by God* and *God Believes in Love: Straight Talk About Gay Marriage* and is the subject of two feature-length documentaries: *For the Bible Tells Me So* and *Love Free or Die*, which won the Special Jury Prize at Sundance. Bishop Robinson was invited by Barack Obama to give the invocation at the opening inaugural ceremonies at the Lincoln Memorial in 2009.

 **Scott Sanders** became a staff verger at Washington National Cathedral following a career focused on HIV/AIDS advocacy and direct service. He was confirmed at the cathedral in 2014 after a decades-long search for a faith community that spoke to his heart and embraced the LGBTQIA community. He has a degree in English from the University of Virginia and completed the Metta Institute's End of Life Practitioner Program. His writing has appeared in diverse sources, including *National Geographic Traveler,* Episcopal Cafe, and AIDS Patient Care, as well as his blog, *Grace Among Us.*

Terri Lynn Simpson is a poet, retreat leader, and the coordinator for the Center for Prayer and Pilgrimage at Washington National Cathedral where she has worked for more than two decades. Celtic spirituality is her path and inviting people into thin places where they may share their stories and experience the presence of the holy is her work. Grounded in the three-fold practices of prayer, pilgrimage, and poetry, she weaves strands of these Celtic influences into the retreats, pilgrimages, and workshops she leads. Terri Lynn has a graduate degree in theology and a doctorate in spirituality and story from Wesley Theological Seminary.

Torrence N. Thomas serves as head cathedral verger at Washington National Cathedral. He is primarily responsible for supporting the bishop, dean, and cathedral clergy in carrying out their priestly functions. He holds a doctorate in medieval history from Yale University and has studied at Duke, Oxford, and New York universities. His professional experience includes positions at the National Gallery of Art, the Folger Shakespeare Library, the Beinecke Rare Book and Manuscript Library, and the Rubinstein Rare Book Library.

About the Photographer _____

Danielle E. Thomas served as Washington National Cathedral's principal photographer from 2013-2021. She regularly captured the cathedral's worship and programmatic life, national services, and architecture. A graduate of Indiana University and Georgetown University, her photography has appeared in *The New York Times, The Washington Post*, and other major publications. She is now based in Louisville, Kentucky, and you can see more of her work on Instagram @cameradroll.

About Forward Movement_____

Forward Movement is committed to inspiring disciples and empowering evangelists. Our ministry is lived out by creating resources such as books, small-group studies, apps, and conferences.

Our daily devotional, *Forward Day by Day*, is also available in Spanish (*Adelante día a día*) and Braille, online, as a podcast, and as an app for smartphones or tablets. It is mailed to more than fifty countries, and we donate nearly tens of thousands of copies each quarter to prisons, hospitals, and nursing homes. We actively seek partners across the church and look for ways to provide resources that inspire and challenge.

A ministry of the Episcopal Church for more than eighty years, Forward Movement is a nonprofit organization funded by sales of resources and by gifts from generous donors.

To learn more about Forward Movement and our resources, visit ForwardMovement.org. We are delighted to be doing this work and invite your prayers and support.